ASHWOOD

A NOVEL

Todd Crawshaw

CrowsnestPublishing.com

ASHWOOD

All Rights Reserved.

No part of this publication
may be reproduced
or transmitted in any form whatsoever
without written permission
except in the case of brief quotations
with reference to source.

Visit: www.toddcrawshaw.com

ISBN: 979-8-9882757-4-9

Copyright © 2025 Todd Crawshaw
First Edition

Cover design by author

CrowsnestPublishing.com

Printed in the United States of America

IN

MEMORY OF

A GIRL

WHO WAS

AND COULD

HAVE BEEN

ALSO BY TODD CRAWSHAW

NOVELS

Goddess: Son of Medusa

The Center's Edge Revisited

Portrait of a Rainbow as a Young Man

God, Sex & Psychosis

Heretofore

Exploits of the Satyr

SHORT STORIES & POEMS

Light-Years in the Dark

Naked Lies and the Truth

STAGE PLAYS & SCREENPLAYS

Amulet

Retreat

Liability

ASHWOOD

PART 1

ASHWOOD

ASHWOOD

And I find it kinda funny
I find it kinda sad
The dreams in which I'm dying
Are the best I've ever had
I find it hard to tell you
I find it hard to take
When people run in circles
It's a very, very mad world
— Tears for Fears

ASHWOOD

OBITUARY

Cassandra (Cassy) Crow, was laid to rest yesterday at Fernwood Cemetery, Mill Valley, California after her skeletal remains were discovered at South Jetty Beach in Oregon, following her seven-year disappearance. She is believed to be the final victim in a series of murders that shocked the art world. Cassandra was born in Eugene, Oregon. A self-proclaimed teenage runaway, she hitch-hiked to San Francisco during the Summer of Love where she remained, eventually marrying, and raised a family in Marin county. Art World Magazine named Cassandra Crow "Queen of the Canvas." She was also featured on the cover of TIME magazine for her unique oil paintings, ranging in style from surreal portraits to her art in humanistic expressionism. She described her meteoric rise to fame as accidental and not of her making, nor her desire. "My wish is for solitude and anonymity," she told a reporter days before her disappearance. This statement, desiring seclusion, belied a deeper truth. "Cassy was a wild child," said a friend who knew her during the sixties and seventies. "She was a dichotomy, an enigma, a free spirit." Cassandra is survived by her husband, Aaron Ashwood, son Blaise, twin daughters, Sky and Iris, grandsons, Logan and Flynn, and granddaughters Cora and Birdie. A Celebration of Life will be held in San Francisco's Golden Gate Park Polo Fields on Saturday, May 9th. Anyone who wishes to attend is welcome.

ASHWOOD

CHAPTER 1

Euphoria. That was the sensation of pleasure he was feeling. The warmth of her sparkling face. A smile full of love. Her appearance hovering before him dreamlike, pressing her lips into his, lingering there as their bodies became one.

He felt her magic again. How could she be dead?

"Grandpa? Are you in there? Knock-knock."

Ashwood opened his eyes. He saw the girl he loved and had lost. He blinked, confused by her playful giggle, before recognizing her to be his granddaughter, Birdie.

For a moment he forgot he was paralyzed, locked in the prison of his body, the result of a stroke. In his mind he smiled, wanting to tell her what a joy she was to behold, how much she reminded him of Cassy. But he couldn't move his muscles. He vaguely recalled the onslaught of the headache, followed by a strange warmth turning his head into melting wax, numbing his face, his arms, his legs, until the collapse into darkness. Upon awakening, he was slow to grasp the reality of his situation. Lying upright on a hospital bed, unable to move, he found himself being spoken to by doctors and nurses as though he had regressed to an infant, a newborn, establishing facial recognition and trying to comprehend this new dimension of life.

"Are you okay? Can you hear me? Blink if you can."

Ashwood blinked at Birdie.

"Everyone is starting to arrive. I can wheel you into the living room if you'd like. Mom says it's okay. Would you like me to?"

Ashwood blinked again.

"Awesome. Give me just a sec."

Birdie looked at her twelve-year-old self in the mirror, bunching her blonde hair, pulling it to the side, and tying it into a ponytail with a sparkly-green scrunchie. She petted the fuzzy-white reindeer on the front of her red sweater as if it was a real animal then turned back to face her grandfather.

"I feel kinda stupid wearing this. Dad bought it for me, thinking I'd like it. He still sees me as a little girl who plays with Little Ponies and dolls. That's not me anymore. But it's Christmas. So I have to wear it. Right? Do you think I look stupid?"

Ashwood blinked and Birdie burst into giggles.

"I love you, Grandpa."

As she checked to make sure his body harness was secure before moving him, she recalled how he used to toss her into the air when she was young. She would shriek with laughter, knowing she'd be caught, then tossed again. She tightened his support-vest straps.

"Is that too tight? I'm not hurting you, am I?"

Ashwood shut his eyes to indicate, no.

Her grandfather's regular live-in caregiver had three days off to be with her family, given that it was Christmas. Birdie volunteered to look after him until the temporary nurse her parents had arranged to come help later in the day arrived. She stepped on the brake release unlocking the wheels and took hold of the handles in the back which had emergency hand breaks. Birdie began to push him forward. "Okay. Off we go."

Birdie bit down on her lower lip, fighting back tears, trying to stay happy. It was Christmas. Her favorite holiday, bringing family members together again. But she felt sad. Sad for her grandfather as she wheeled him down the ramp connecting his part of the house to the next section of the multi-structured home. Originally, his home. One he remodeled himself, along with her Grandma Cassy, whom

Birdie never got to know but lingered like magic fairy dust when she saw certain objects, especially while she stared at her paintings. She knew the history of this house because she was curious about these things. Her parents said she was precocious, a word she had to google to know its meaning. Meaning she had heightened abilities, like those of an adult. But she found that hard to believe because she was only a kid, not even a teenager yet. Curious, that was all. Because their house was the strangest conglomeration of beauty she had ever seen. It was nothing like the homes of her friends.

Her grandpa's section of the house was once lived in by an uncle she never knew – her grandma's older brother who too was disabled. It was constructed specifically for him, along with all the ramps and bridges connecting the separate parts. And now her grandfather was confined to live there too. Birdie stopped to wipe away a tear.

"Look, Grandpa. A squirrel."

She turned his wheelchair. They were midway along a bridge. Beneath them was a meandering brook bordered with river rocks, and beyond, on both sides was lush greenery and tall trees.

"Do you see him?"

Birdie bent down and saw his eyes blink twice.

"He could be a she, I suppose. Anyway, let's keep going. Listen, I hear a car coming up the driveway."

It was midmorning, the sky full of breaking fog within the dense forest of surrounding redwood trees. They passed an outdoor patio area off the main house. It was constructed of rockwork with wood flooring. A redwood burl bar stood under an overhang with massive logs for beams. As they approached the end of the bridge, Birdie saw through the glass walls their Christmas tree lit up in all its glory. Her dad was inside building a fire in the stone hearth.

Birdie stopped and stepped on a button that triggered the sliding glass doors to open. She pushed him into the living room.

"Merry Christmas, Grandpa."

ASHWOOD

CHAPTER 2

1967

Cassy walked through the open door to the Sigma Chi fraternity, located a block from the University of Oregon campus, and into its vacant entryway that smelled of beer, trash, and cigarettes. It was early Saturday morning. She spotted the aftermath signs of a Friday-night party. She peered into the mess hall with long metal tables and chairs, then walked down a hallway into the living room area with a high ceiling and stone partition that housed a fireplace, creating two sections.

The first section was empty. The second section produced three boys slumped in chairs and a sofa, muttering to one another, nursing hangovers, it appeared to Cassy by their demeanor.

"Anyone headed to San Francisco?"

Her unexpected voice woke them from their lethargy.

"Who wants to know?"

Twisting her lips from the wiseass remark, Cassy stated, "I do. Obviously. Any takers?"

One boy straightened up, gazing at her as if at an apparition. She wore black jeans with ripped holes displaying portions of her skin and a tie-dyed t-shirt with the word "LOVE" seen through the opening of her un-zipped leather jacket. Straps over her shoulders held a small backpack. Her black boots matched her coat. A shiny black feather was stuck in the nest of her long blonde hair.

"How old are you?"

She ignored the guy's remark and focused on the one who had taken immediate interest in her. "Why does it matter?"

"It matters. What are you, twelve or thirteen?"

"Fuck off. I'm *fifteen*. Forget it." She turned and left.

"Wait!"

Cassy stopped and turned back. The guy whose attention she had hooked rose to his feet. He approached her in the hallway.

"Okay. I'm waiting. What?"

"Why do you want to go to San Francisco?"

"It's gotta be more fun than being here. So I've heard."

"I'm from there."

"San Francisco? Why would you want to be here?"

He grinned and gestured to the surroundings. "College."

"Right. Anyway…"

"Let's talk."

Cassy hitched both hands around the straps of her backpack and took a moment to look him over as if she were browsing at a car lot, interested in buying, checking out his features, wondering if he was reliable, wouldn't break down easily, and gave good mileage.

"Do you have a name?"

"Aaron. Ashwood."

"Cassy. Crow." She touched her black feather.

"Crow? Seriously?"

"*Caw*," she squawked with a droll smile.

Aaron laughed. "Come with me."

"Why?"

"It's gotta be more fun than staying here. I have a car."

Cassy twisted her lips, considering his offer, wondering if he was someone who might try to rape her.

Aaron read her hesitation. "You can trust me."

"You're trustworthy?"

"I am. I won't try to rape you."

"That's a shame," she teased.

Aaron grinned. "You're something else. Come on."

"Where are we going?"

"For a ride?"

※

Cassy stared at the tarnished blue, funny-looking station wagon as Aaron opened the driver's door, which made a creaking noise, and sat inside, waiting for her to decide on whether to enter. After a full fifteen seconds, she removed her backpack, opened the side door and plopped down onto the passenger seat.

"What kind of car is this?"

"Peugeot 403. It's a classic."

"You're joking."

"I am. Do you like it?"

She frowned, peering behind where the back seats would be but folded down to accommodate a mattress across the back, along with cushions and a couple of blankets. Both side windows were covered with blue tie-dyed curtains. The sight of the bed gave her a queasy feeling which she tried to suppress.

"Far out. So you're a hippie."

"Hardly. Maybe."

"Your hair is too short." She studied his features. "You're more like a James Dean type. Or, hum, Steve McQueen?"

"You don't know me. Are these your action heroes?"

"No. My brother's obsessed with them. He made me watch all their movies."

"How old is your brother?"

"Nineteen."

"Ah, same as me."

"You're not the same. He's bigger and taller."

"I meant in age."

"So you're not a hippie?"

"I haven't decided what I am. You?"

"I'm a runaway."

He wasn't sure if it was a joke. "Where are you from?"

"Eugene."

Aaron laughed and started the engine. "You haven't gotten very far yet."

"Call it a trial run. Are we driving to San Francisco?"

"No."

"Then where?"

"Where would you like to go?"

"San Francisco."

"Hendricks Park, maybe? To a beach?"

"I've never been to the ocean."

Aaron backed out of the parking space in the fraternity lot and stopped the car. "I don't believe you."

"It's true."

"Convince me. It's less than an hour's drive from here."

"Fine. Let's go." Cassy repositioned the backpack in her lap, her fingers fiddling with the zipper. "I said, let's go, already."

Aaron shook his head, grinning, shifting from reverse into first gear, and drove out of the fraternity parking lot. "You've lived here all your life and you've never been to the ocean? For a runaway, you haven't seen a lot."

"Don't judge me." Cassy twirled a strand of her long hair with her index finger. "I've been plenty of places. Just not the ocean. My father was in the Navy. He hated it. He says he never wants to see the ocean ever again. Convinced?"

"What about with your friends, other families? Didn't—"

"I don't make friends. I'm more of a loner."

"No boyfriends?"

Cassy gave Aaron a hard, sharp look. "Do I look like the kind of person who has boyfriends?"

"Yes. Is there something wrong with you?"

"Let's talk about something else. Or nothing at all."

※

Cassy went silent as Aaron drove. She was reassessing all the things she had tossed into her backpack. Along with spare clothing and three candy bars, she was glad she brought a knife. It was her brother's prized switchblade, which he showed her once, which he never used, so she stole it. She knew he'd forgive her. He was always looking out for her. Having his knife meant he was somehow there to protect her. That was how she rationalized the theft. She loved her older brother. He would listen to her complaints. Unlike her father, who responded by yelling and grounding her, posting news articles on her bedroom door about girls being raped and murdered, each time she threatened to run away from home.

"What are you running away from?"

The broken silence woke Cassy from her random thoughts.

"From home. Duh."

"Yeah, but why? What's going on? You're only fifteen."

"What does my age have to do with anything?"

"Fair point. Are you being abused at—"

"No. I hate school, for *one*."

"And two?"

Cassy unzipped her backpack. "Two, I hate my father. After I got suspended from high school, twice, he talked my mother into transferring me to an all-girls catholic school, where I'm forced to wear a stupid uniform. If I get kicked out of there, he says they'll place me in a military school for girls. He wants to break me down and strip away all that is me. I despise him. Okay?"

"Why did you get suspended?"

"For cutting school. I snuck off to hear a band play one afternoon at your college. Someone ratted on me. Then, yeah, a teacher caught me getting high in the girls bathroom."

Aaron glanced over at her. "Smoking pot?"

Cassy smirked. "No. Shooting heroin. Yes, smoking a stupid joint. Big deal. But that got me kicked out for good."

"What are you doing?"

Cassy had shifted herself around to lean against the door. In her hand was a pencil. Resting on her backpack was a sketch pad.

"I'm going to draw you."

Aaron glanced over and saw Fern Ridge Lake through the side window where Cassy was resting her head. She didn't seem to notice or care about the passing view, focused solely on him as she moved her pencil very intently across the paper. "So, you're an artist."

"I'm an artist. And you're my subject. Stop looking at me. Eyes on the road."

"We should reach the coast in about thirty minutes."

"I should have you drawn by then."

"How long have you—"

"Stop talking." Cassy brought the pencil to her mouth, biting the eraser as she studied his face. "You have good features."

"Thanks."

"Now keep quiet and stay still while I draw you."

Cassy looked at Aaron, then through the windshield. "Why are we stopping?"

"We have options."

"Options?"

Aaron had pulled off to the side of the road and was pointing at the signs ahead. "Pick a beach. South Jetty Beach, South Siuslaw Jetty, or North Jetty Beach?"

"Which one is the nicest?"

"They're all nice."

"Which is the closest?"

"South Jetty."

"Let's go there."

A few minutes later, Aaron drove the Peugeot onto a portion of the beach, parking the car within a secluded sand dune overlooking the ocean with its breaking waves a short distance away.

She nodded at the view. "Pretty cool."

"A rather blasé response at seeing the ocean your first time."

"I lied. I've been to the ocean and beaches before."

"So you're an artist *and* a liar."

"Pretty much. That sums me up. Yep."

Aaron laughed. "Can I see what you drew?"

Cassy handed over her sketch pad.

Aaron's eyes widened. "Wow. That's how you see me?"

"No. It's who you are."

"You made me look better than I actually am."

"Nobody sees themselves the way others do. Give it back."

Aaron began flipping through her sketchbook. "Jesus! Damn, you're really talented. You drew all these faces?"

Cassy snatched back her drawings. "No. *Jesus* did."

"I meant it as a compliment."

"Thanks. I want to get my feet wet. Are you game?"

Cassy unlaced and removed her combat boots, then her socks. She opened the door and ran, hopping over a tuft of grass, and down the gentle slope of sand, screaming wildly and waving her arms.

Aaron sat for a moment, watching as she ran away.

ASHWOOD

CHAPTER 3

Aaron walked barefoot in the sand, following after Cassy who was now running back and forth, chasing after the breaking waves. Having rolled up the bottoms of her black jeans, she let the saltwater swirl around her ankles. She danced, splashing herself with abandon, almost maniacally, putting on a show for him. He smiled at her, though wondered what the fuck he was thinking. Driving a fifteen-year-old runaway to the beach. A girl he knew nothing about. Who was she? What was she? She didn't seem quite real.

He questioned his motives. Did he have a motive? It felt more like she was calling the shots, leading him astray, as if hypnotically. He'd been drawn by her strange energy. And, of course, her beauty. She was gorgeous but in a dark and devious, potentially dangerous, embodiment of a mythical spritely water nymph. As he approached her, she startled him by leaping onto his body, grasping him with her arms and legs – like the tentacles of an octopus who were known to be playful and inquisitive. She laughed and let go, dropping back to her feet before he had time to respond or know what to make of her impromptu actions.

He became aroused. She was playing with his emotions. She was teasing him, and he liked it, whatever she was doing. She grabbed his hand, pulling him toward the ocean. He was willing to let her take them both into the waves, underwater, but she stopped short as the saltwater crashed and rushed around their legs, soaking them both. He looked at her shocked expression and they burst into laughter. She squeezed his hand.

"I think I might like you. Look. We have the beach to ourselves. Almost. Now I want to get warm."

Aaron took note of the overcast sky and the sparsely populated coastline. Cassy held onto his hand, pulling him back toward the car. She kicked at the sand, flinging tiny shells in the air with her toes as they meandered along.

"I'm having fun. This was a good idea of yours."

"Better than driving to San Francisco?"

"I didn't say that."

"Are you still planning on running away?"

"I haven't decided. I'm living in the moment. So don't go and burst my bubble of happiness."

Cassy opened the passenger side door, took her backpack and tossed it into the back. She opened the next door and crawled onto the mattress. "Get in, already. It's cold outside."

"My pants are soaking wet."

"Take them off. What's the big deal?"

Aaron unbuttoned and stepped out of his jeans. He draped his pants over the rounded hood of his car. He opened the back door and climbed onto the mattress as Cassy whistled comically.

"Look at you in your bright red boxers. We match."

Cassy had removed her pants and was busy taking out another pair of black jeans from her backpack. She wore red underwear and handed Aaron her wet pants.

"Place mine across the hood too, please."

Aaron obliged, laying her jeans next to his, then returned.

"The heated metal from the engine plus the sun, when it breaks, might dry them by the end of day."

"Whatever. Sorry I caused you to wet your pants," she said, wiggling into her dry spare. "You're not embarrassed, are you?"

Aaron crawled onto the mattress "Should I be?"

"Do you wanna smoke a joint?"

Cassy removed a hand-rolled cigarette from her backpack as if magically pulling a rabbit from a hat, displaying it theatrically.

"Ta-da! Does your cigarette lighter work? Wait. I think I packed matches too. I did. Super smart of me."

Sitting on the mattress in his red boxers, Aaron was handed the cannabis after Cassy sucked in smoke, holding her breath.

"Unexpected," said Aaron, inhaling, coughing, and handing the thinly-rolled spliff back to Cassy.

She blew out a plume of smoke. "What? Us getting high?"

"I get the feeling nothing about you should surprise me." Aaron smiled and reached for a folded blanket by the rear door and draped it over his legs.

"Getting cold or shy?"

He took another hit of marijuana. "A little of both."

"No need to be shy." She drew in more smoke, then pinched the burning end with her thumb and fingertip. "We should save the rest for later. It's pretty potent."

Aaron nodded, sensing the intoxicant blossoming exponentially inside his head, suddenly making him self-conscious.

"Hum," said Cassy. "Want to see something cool? She didn't wait for his answer as she rummaged inside her pack and took out a narrow black and silver object. "Observe." She pressed a button and the switchblade spung to life, startling Aaron's stoned mental state as he stared at the sharp jack-in-the-box knife.

"*Shit*. What do you have that for?"

"For protection. In case I need to defend myself against some weirdo perv." She pushed down the blade and slipped the knife into her backpack. Reaching for a pillow to position behind her back, she noticed a small leather bag next to the metal bulge that formed one of the wheel wells. She pointed.

"What's in there?"

"My camera."

"You take photos?"

"That's what a camera does."

"Wiseass. Let me see. Show me."

Aaron unzipped the bag and removed his Pentax Spotmatic.

"Is that your major? Photography?"

"More a minor. A hobby. I like to use only natural light."

"What do you photograph?"

"People, mainly."

"Take a picture of me. It's only fair. I drew your face."

Aaron adjusted the aperture and shutter speed. "The light's not very good in here."

"I pulled a knife on you. Now you have to shoot me."

Aaron grinned and aimed the camera at her. He laughed as she distorted her face. He took her photo. "Come on. I want to capture the real you."

"This is the real me. Fine." She dropped her smile and leaned against the car wall, staring back, holding a relaxed pose.

Aaron clicked off several shots.

"What do you study at the college?"

"I got accepted into the School of Architecture."

"I guess that means you like to design and build things."

"Pretty much. When I was a kid, I constructed an elaborate tree house in our backyard."

"Sisters and brothers?"

"I'm an only child."

Cassy removed two Snickers bars, tossing one to Aaron, then gazed around at their cozy enclosure with its curved roof ceiling and side windows covered with curtains. "I like what you've done with the place. What should we do now?"

"Talk?"

Aaron couldn't recall what they talked about – everything and nothing – while ensconced like vagabonds on a semi-isolated beach, the sky overcast with emerging openings of sunlight. The constant voice of the ocean washed rhythmically against the shore the entire time. It seemed to be echoing their raw emotions that poured forth, exposed and unfiltered. They explored each other's minds and bared their souls. Sharing secrets. All that they hated. All that they loved.

Cassy asked, "Do you think there's a god?"

"Probably. There must be something else beyond us."

"Why?"

"Just a feeling. But nothing we can ever comprehend."

"You're saying God is incomprehensible?"

"Exactly," said Aaron. "We're not supposed to know. That's the holy mystery of life. Our inexplicable human conundrum."

"Hum," said Cassy, considering, sucking the last bit of smoke from the roach pinched between her fingernails. "Ouch. Shit." She dropped and crushed out what was left before the remnants burned a hole in the mattress. "No harm. Do you know what I think?"

"I realize I come across as someone who is psychic, but I'm not. So, no, to your question. I have no clue what's going on inside your beautiful head."

"Fuck off," she laughed. "Wait. You think I'm beautiful?"

"Yes. An *ungodly* vision. You are a true beauty."

"I don't see myself as beautiful."

"Well, you are. Now tell me what you were thinking."

"I forgot. No, now I remember. I zoned out for a second. I think I'm really stoned."

"I could have deciphered that."

"If, somehow, we were able to comprehend who and what this thing called god is… like, you know, see God, the meaning of life, we would go insane."

"What?"

"Our minds would be blown, unable to handle the truth."

"Wow. I think you might be right."

"You don't think it's stupid, what I said?"

"No. That's heavy. I think it's kind of profound."

They were reclined against opposite sides of the station wagon, slumped down on the mattress. Cassy reached toward him and took hold of his hand. She stroked his palm with her thumb. Aaron felt his body tingle from her touch, causing a warm sensation to travel up his arm, bursting throughout his body, arousing his heart.

He joked, "Are you a palm reader now?"

"Yes, I am." She pulled his hand closer, palm raised, her index finger tracing the folds in his skin. "I'm sensing a strong premonition that your pants are dry."

Aaron laughed and pulled back his hand. "You're also a tease, aren't you?"

"Go fetch your pants."

Aaron removed the blanket covering his legs and swiveled on his rear end to open the door and exit the car.

Cassy cat-whistled. "Amazing ass. A true beauty."

Aaron glanced back with a curt smile. "Like I said."

"About me?"

The sun was setting over the ocean. Aaron returned wearing his jeans. He held Cassy's pants too and tossed them beside her as he climbed back inside. "That did the trick. They're now toasty warm, thanks to the sun god."

"Scoot over here. Let me feel." She placed a hand on his thigh, rubbing the fabric. "When were you planning to kiss me?"

"Is that what you want?"

"I'm never sure what I want. Kiss me. Then I'll know."

They leaned toward each other and their lips met. What began as a tentative, exploratory touching of the flesh, quickly turned into a passionate hunger for more. They pulled into one another and fell sideways onto the mattress, pausing a moment to breathe.

"You're a good kisser," said Cassy, licking her lips. "This could get us into trouble."

The waning sunlight broke through an opening in the curtain to shine on Cassy's eyes. "Do you realize you have the most amazing irises? Iridescent green circled in black. Absolutely stunning."

"And I just realized you've grown bigger since we first met."

He frowned at her teasing smile. Her fingers touched his swollen crotch and he pulled away.

"We shouldn't be doing this."

"Why not?"

"You're fifteen."

"I think we've established *that*. So what?"

"You're right. This could lead to trouble." His thoughts went to statutory rape and the repercussions for acting stupid, for letting his inflamed libido highjack any rational thinking.

Cassy squinted at his reluctance to keep kissing her. "I wasn't asking you to fuck me. Although. Wait. Are you still a virgin?"

"No."

"I am. When did you lose your virginity?"

"Why do you want to know?"

"I'm curious. Be honest with me."

"Sixteen."

"With who? Your first girlfriend?"

"No. Nothing like that."

"Like what? Tell me." She rested her head against her arm.

"At a brothel in the Nevada desert."

"No. A whore house?"

"Yes."

"What was it like?"

"Jesus, Cassy. I don't know. It was okay. Awkward."

"Not fun?"

"I wouldn't say that. I was drunk. So were my friends. There was talk of his place called Mustang Ranch. So we decided to go and check out what it would be like."

Cassy giggled. "To have sex with a horse?"

"Right." He smiled, shrugging off any embarrassment. "I mean, it was an adventure. The woman was in her thirties. It was over fast. Not very memorable."

"Or romantic? Am I making you uncomfortable?"

"Why would I be uncomfortable talking about my sex life with a fifteen-year-old girl I just met and barely know?"

"You're only four years older than me, Aaron."

"It's like dog years when you're a teenager. And legal penalties, like jail time, when you cross the line for unaccepted behavior."

"For kissing me? Wow. Have you ever had sex with someone your own age?"

"Sure. But with no one I've felt true feelings of love for."

"Like me?" She fluttered her eyelashes.

The realization struck him suddenly. "Yes, actually."

"I've decided I want to lose my virginity to you."

"Cassy."

"Not now. Tonight I just want you to kiss me and tell me you love me. Can we continue doing that?"

"I should be taking you home. Before it gets too late."

"No! Don't burst my happiness bubble. I'm not going home yet. Maybe never."

"Then you'll get us both into trouble."

"My parents aren't worried. I told them I was sleeping over at a friend's house tonight."

"You told me you don't make friends."

"I have friends."

"I don't know what to believe anymore."

"You can take me home tomorrow morning. I promise."

"Can I trust you to keep—"

"Yes. Now kiss me and tell me how much you love me. I need you right now. This is for us. To be *memorable*."

Cassy began to cry. Aaron held her, consoling her as they kissed. He realized, without a doubt, that he had fallen madly in love with this enigma of a girl. It was a passion he had never felt before. There was desperation in her embrace, an exposed vulnerability she'd been concealing, surging now like an opened floodgate. The emotional neediness was a need he sensed in himself too, a need for her love. He didn't want whatever this was, whatever they had, to ever end. They continued to kiss and snuggle together as if wanting to become one being inside a warm cocoon, kissing late into the night until the early morning came.

ASHWOOD

CHAPTER 4

Cassy was silent and sullen on the drive back to Eugene. Unlike the drive to the beach, her eyes avoided Aaron, staring out the side window at the passing scenery. He could feel her unease, her anxiety, her sense of freedom eroding. Aaron felt complicit, as though about to deliver her into police custody to serve a prison sentence.

She was biting her fingernails.

"Did you want to talk?"

"No," she muttered into the pane of glass.

He saw her tears reflected in the window. She brushed at them furtively with the back of her hand. Her demeanor was the antithesis of the assertive girl he first saw stride into the Sigma Chi fraternity, asking if anyone would drive her to San Francisco.

"I know you wanted to run away from home, Cassy. But that's extreme. Maybe you can work things out with your dad, if—"

"It's not your problem, Aaron."

"I want to help. Should I meet your parents?"

"God, no!" She abruptly turned her head. "Are you crazy? My father would kill you. Then me."

"You didn't say you were sleeping over at a friends, did you?"

"It doesn't matter."

The deflated image of herself came to life as Cassy sucked in air, sat up, and regained her posture. "Fuck it. I can deal with whatever happens. My father doesn't own me. It's my life, not his."

"If you need me, you know where to find me. Here."

Cassy looked over at Aaron holding out a piece of paper. "It's the number at the fraternity house. Call me if you need me."

"I need you." She took the scrap of paper and stuffed it in her backpack. "Are we still in love?"

"Undeniably. Somehow we're going to make this work."

"Ha. Says the nineteen-year-old to the fifteen-year-old. Yeah, well, we're almost there."

"What's your street address?"

"Turn here. Then the next left. It's the blue house at the end of the culdesac."

"You're shitting me," said Aaron. "You live only a few blocks away from the Sigma Chi house?"

"Pull up to the curb and drop me off fast."

Aaron stopped the car. Cassy lunged over at him, kissing him on the lips, grabbed her backpack straps, then opened the door. At the sight of a large man standing outside her front door, she froze.

"Get inside this house! Now! Who the hell is that?"

Through the back window, Aaron glimpsed the presumed father pointing at his car, shouting at Cassy. Their voices faded as he drove away and Aaron felt guilt-ridden for abandoning her.

Cassy ran into the house with her father close behind, slamming shut the door. "Stay where you are, young lady!"

Cassy stopped and looked back. "What?"

"Explain yourself. Where the hell have you been?"

"I went to the beach, okay?"

"Not okay! Goddammit, Cassy! You had your mother worried sick not knowing where you were. She had me driving all over town and calling your friends. You can't run off like that."

"Sorry." She turned to walk away.

"Who was he? That man in the car who dropped you off?"

"Just a boy I met."

"Just a *boy* you met? Who?"

"At a fraternity house. We drove to the beach for the day."

"And stayed the night! Where?"

"We slept in his station wagon. It was no big deal."

"You're grounded. Permanently!"

Cassy glanced over at her mother standing by the kitchen, her hand over her mouth. She saw her big brother standing in the hall, remaining silent too, shaking his head.

"Look at me," said her father. "Did he touch you? Force you to do things?"

"No. Like what?"

"You *know* what, damn it. He turned to his wife. "Mary, phone Doctor Stevens to schedule an emergency vaginal inspection on our daughter now!"

"No!" screamed Cassy. "Dad, nothing happened!"

"I don't believe you. I want his name."

"Who?"

"The one you *slept* with."

"We didn't have sex! We *kissed*, that's all."

"I'm through with you, Cassy. Be a tramp, for all I care." He slammed his fist against the wall. "Mary, you deal with our little slut of a daughter. I'm finished with her."

"I hate you! I was running away from home. That's right. I was. And I should have *never* come back!"

Her father stared at her, dismissively.

"But Aaron, he talked me into returning."

"His name is Aaron? I want a last name."

"Fuck you!" Cassy ran down the hall, past her brother, and opened her bedroom door, glancing back. "Aaron's sweet and funny. A good person. A better person than you'll ever be! I hate you!"

She slammed her door shut.

"God damn you!"

Her father was stopped by her brother who stood in his way, his hand held out. At six foot three, Victor looked down at his father. As if to a child throwing a tantrum, he calmly said, "Dad, let Mom talk to Cassy. Okay? What you're doing isn't helping."

Their father chewed at his lower lip, then moved away.

*

Cassy heard a quiet knocking on her bedroom door.

"Go away! Leave me alone!"

"Cassy? It's only me."

Her mother found Cassy lying face down on her bed crying into her pillow, the backpack thrown onto the floor. Mary sat on the edge of the bed, touching her daughter, rubbing her back.

"Tell me what happened?"

"Nothing. *Nothing* happened. Aaron was good to me."

"I believe you, Birdie."

Cassy looked up from her pillow, at the sound of her pet name spoken, the one her mother used to call her when she was a child learning to walk, riding a bike, climbing a tree. She smiled, wiping snot from her nose. "I'm sorry I made you worry."

"I know you want to fly away. But you're still so young. Stay in the nest a little longer. Please?"

"Why is Dad so mean? He's the one who makes me want to run away from home."

"He wasn't always like this."

"The tumor, you mean?"

Mary nodded. "Try to remember how your daddy used to be. How lovely he was before the operation. He lost everything, Cassy. Try to understand how that can change a proud man like your father. He owned and ran that auto dealership where he's now a salesman, who isn't good with people anymore. The new owners, his previous employees, keep him employed out of loyalty for who he once was. Imagine that kind of loss. He still loves you. He doesn't know how to give that right kind of love anymore."

Cassy tried to imagine an alternative world, one where she lived within a happy family, in which her father hadn't been lobotomized, and now half-functioning like he belonged to the walking dead.

"I hate going to that stupid new school."

"I know you do. Just try your best to stay out of more trouble. Your wild behavior is not helping the situation. It only adds fuel to the fire. Understand? I will try to reason with your father."

Her mom kissed her forehead and left.

Cassy rolled onto her back and stared at the blank ceiling. She looked at the bare white walls. She hadn't even bothered to hang any posters after they moved into this soulless tract house when they lost their other house. She spread her arms across the bed, imagining the images of Jesus displayed crucified on crosses, painted on the school walls, also carved into statues with his tortured expression looking down on all the girls passing in their uniforms of pleated skirts and starched-white blouses. She pictured the sight of them like insects, seen from above, walking in crazy-eight patterns around the campus, their minds being filled with illusions of a perfect world, somewhere inside an invented heaven, if only they prayed to a God and believed. She wanted to scream. She was on the verge of more tears when she heard another knock.

"Go away."

"No way, Sis," said her brother in a deep voice as he entered her room. He raised his arms like Frankenstein's monster, making her laugh, recalling the memories of her towering brother mechanically chasing her around the house. He sat on the corner of her bed.

"You really know how to push Dad's button and set him off."

"Hi, Vic. I stole your switchblade. Forgive me?"

"Keep it if you want."

"When do you leave to work at that ski resort in Tahoe?"

"In a couple weeks."

"You won't be here to protect me then."

"You won't need me. Dad's all bluff. He's not going to hurt you. Plus, you now have my knife."

Cassy grinned. Victor lightly squeezed her ankle.

"So tell me about this guy you slept with."

"Fuck off. We just kissed."

"Was he any good?"

Cassy closed her eyes. "He was better than good."

After the solitude of the ocean and the warm embrace of Cassy, the taste of her lips fresh in his mind, Aaron entered the din of the fraternity house, which sounded like an institutional insane asylum. Breakfast was being served in the mess hall and the racket assaulted his senses. He avoided saying anything to anyone as he ran two steps at a time up the stairs to the room he shared, desks and mattresses at opposite sides of the walls.

His roommate's first words were, "What the hell, man?"

"Good to see you too, Brad."

"You took that fifteen-year old somewhere, didn't you?"

"We went to the beach."

"Are you out of your fucking mind?"

"Apparently." He tried to lighten things. "Jury's still out."

"I'm serious. Her father came here looking for her, and asking questions. I said I knew nothing about any missing girl. But Harvey said he saw her leave with you."

"I dropped her off at her house a few minutes ago."

"Expect the cops to be showing up anytime soon."

"Nothing happened. We didn't have sex or anything."

"Tell that to the police. Then to a jury."

Aaron began to pace. "Fuck. I *am* an idiot."

"What if she lies, and tells them an opposite story?"

"Cassy wouldn't do that."

"Cassy?" Brad huffed. "You trust that girl not to lie?"

"Fuck. Fuck. *Fuck.*"

"That's a word I'd avoid using when you're questioned."

Aaron broke into a sweat. He collapsed upon the floor mattress he called his bed. He shut his eyes and felt sick to his stomach. All that had tasted so pure and sweet before turned sour. He mentally fought against the negativity, refusing to believe what he'd done and how he felt for Cassy was wrong. He wondered, is this why it's called being madly in love?

He closed his eyes and prayed to a god who he wasn't convinced even existed. One that was incomprehensible.

The subsequent weekdays and his college courses went by in a distracted blur. He was incapable of concentrating during his classes or participating in any conversations. In the first days after dropping Cassy off, he worried about being summoned by the police. By the end of the week, he worried that Cassy would never call him.

"No calls from your jail-bait chick?"

Brad's sarcasm, seeing Aaron's face, changed to concern.

"Hey, man. I'm no shrink, but you need to do something. This is destroying you. You know where she lives. Act on it."

Come Saturday, Aaron drove to her blue house. He sat in his car a full minute before pushing himself, resolving to walk up and ring the doorbell. A woman answered the door.

"Hi," he said. "Is Cassy home?"

Her eyes filled with tears. "No, Cassandra is not. She's gone."

"What do you mean, gone?"

"Who are you?"

A man pushed past her in the doorway.

"You're him, aren't you? The prick that abducted her before."

"I never abducted your daughter, Sir."

"I'm her father. I should have you arrested, you little shit!"

"L-listen," Aaron stammered. "I don't know what's going on. Is she alright?"

Another man, the brother, Aaron assumed, taller than both his parents, gently nudged and squeezed past to be in front.

"Are you Aaron?"

"That's right."

"You should come inside. You need to come inside. Please."

Aaron found himself sitting on a sofa, staring across at Cassy's family who were staring back at him.

"Can I get you something?"

"This isn't a fucking social visit, Mary. We're looking to find answers. Cassy's been gone for three days now!"

"She left a note this time. I'm her brother, Victor."

"What did she write?"

"None of your fucking business!"

"Dad. Stop it," scolded Victor. "This isn't helping."

There was something wrong with the father, mentally, Aaron ascertained. He wasn't normal, somehow. His focus tended to drift, distracted by something unseen, as if registering some voice inside his head. He glared at Aaron. "What did you say to me?"

"I didn't say anything." Aaron's palms began to sweat.

The mother seemed at a loss for words, wiping at tears.

Victor reached into his coat pocket and handed Aaron a folded piece of paper. Aaron saw handwriting scribbled in black ink upon opening the textured paper. He recognized it to be a page torn from Cassy's sketchbook. He looked down to read the words:

> *I have run away.*
> *Do not try to find me.*
> *I will not be found.*
> *I have left home for good.*
> *I will always love you Mom,*
> *you are wonderful.*
> *I do not hate you Dad,*
> *for I know you cannot help*
> *being who you are,*
> *and can never be again*
> *who you were.*
> *Victor,*
> *you have always been*
> *my rock of strength,*
> *forever keeping me grounded,*
> *happy, and safe.*
> *Do not blame Aaron*
> *for my disappearance*
> *or ask him where I have gone*
> *because he won't know.*
> *I love you all.*
> *Goodbye,*
> *Cassy*

Aaron looked up from her letter. Cassy's father was muttering to his wife about something, looking befuddled, standing up.

"What did she mean by that? I can't help being who I am. And will never be who I was. It makes no sense. Jesus, Mary, what are we going to do? Our baby girl left us!" Confusion and anger filled his watery eyes. He looked down at Aaron. "This is your damned fault! I don't believe what she wrote about you. Where is she?"

Aaron was numb from shock that Cassy had left him too and handed the letter back to Victor. He knew where Cassy had run off to. San Francisco. It was obvious to him. "I don't know, Sir."

"Liar. Liar!" He stormed away, kicking over an ottoman stool. Mary followed after her husband down the hallway.

Left alone with her brother, Aaron didn't know what to say, or what he would do with himself now. He felt lost. Victor's brooding, resolute eyes were thoughtfully scrutinizing Aaron.

"I can see it now. What she saw in you."

Aaron squinted, looking at her brother's steady smile.

"The McQueen thing. Except I think you're more like a Dean. Aaron, try not to be angry with Cassy and go nuts, okay?"

Same age, but her brother seemed older and wiser than himself. Victor was big, solid, and kind hearted. A loving brother who cared deeply for his sister. He was accepting, resigned to the fact that Cassy had chosen to go, leaving them all behind. Aaron, by contrast, was not so sure about himself, if he could live with this emptiness, this feeling of loss, and find a way to be okay.

Victor told him, "I knew she'd do it, eventually. Cassy's always been headstrong. Free-spirited. Wildly independent. I'm sad, but I trust she'll figure things out and be fine. If it's any consolation, we talked. She told me all about you. She really liked you a lot."

"I thought we had more than that. I really truly loved her."

Victor placed his large hand on Aaron's shoulder.

"I know. Cassy can do that to you."

PART 2

ASHWOOD

Don't ya love her madly?
Don't ya need her badly?
Don't ya love her ways?
Tell me what you say
Don't ya love her madly?
Wanna be her daddy?
Don't ya love her face?
Don't ya love her as she's walkin' out the door?
Like she did one thousand times before
— The Doors

ASHWOOD

CHAPTER 5

2020

Birdie wheeled her grandfather across the living room, stopping briefly in front of their ten-foot-tall Christmas tree for him to view the twinkling lights and colorful ornaments. She turned his wheelchair and moved him over toward her father who was standing next to the fireplace, admiring his work, staring at the blazing pile of logs.

"Great fire, Dad."

"Thanks, Honey. Merry Christmas, Aaron. How are you doing? All good in there?"

Ashwood blinked.

Birdie asked, "Where do you think he'd like to be?"

"Aaron, why don't we move you away from the fire, over there beside that wall. You'll have a better view to watch everyone. Would that be agreeable with you?"

Ashwood blinked.

Birdie wheeled her grandfather to the designated spot, adjusting the chair for the optimum position.

"I think that's my favorite painting by Grandma. I just love it. Don't you love it, Grandpa?"

On the opposite wall above the hearth, Ashwood could now see the large painting. It depicted an ethereal winged figure rising, one of Cassy's later expressionistic visions, explosive with colors, turbulent and disturbingly ambiguous. An angelic woman striving to find light in a dark world? Aaron recalled seeing Cassy standing on a ladder in her studio, brush in hand, manically painting, desperately trying to capture the lost sense of herself.

Ashwood closed his eyes, unable to stop the streaming tears.

"Grandpa, what's the matter? Are you okay?

※

Birdie rushed into their kitchen. Her mother, Iris, was advising the catering company who were delivering the hors d'oeuvres to be served during the afternoon before the holiday dinner.

"Mom, something's wrong with Grandpa. He's crying. I don't know what to do."

Iris acted immediately, keeping hold of a dish towel that she had in her hand, applying steady repeated pressure as if performing CPR on the cloth. She was an admitted worrier, and the responsible one, the sole sibling who took charge by default to orchestrate the funeral arrangements for their mother, then the live-in nursing care provided for their father when he had his massive stroke. Her older brother, Blaise, was brash and assertive, doling out his opinions as the eldest child, but was useless when it came to being there when it mattered. And her twin sister, Sky, was rarely available to help, galavanting around Hollywood, self-absorbed on her quest to become a star.

"Dad, what's going on?" She dabbed at his tears with the dish towel. He had stopped crying but she crouched down to be eye level with her father. "Is there something I can do for you?"

Ashwood shut his eyes.

"You'll be okay?"

Ashwood blinked.

"What's going on with Dad?"

Iris stood, hearing the voice of her brother. He leaned down to peck her cheek with a kiss. He was dressed in a grey suit and reeked of too much cologne.

"Dad was crying. Something set him off."

Blaise looked down at their father, "Can you blame him? I'd be depressed as hell too if I was paralyzed in a wheelchair. Hi, Dad. The whole gang is here to greet you this time."

He indicated his wife, Nora, standing beside him. She was tall, trained to be statuesque, having worked as a runway model. Blaise had chased many girls, but became obsessed with Nora, pursuing her for a year before she conceded to marry him. They'd been separated twice and divorced once. Resently they'd reconciled and remarried.

Birdie was intrigued by Nora. Her black dress had sparkles, her black hair was long, and her lips thin, rarely smiling.

"Hello, Iris," said Nora. "And to you, too, little bird."

"I'm Birdie."

"I know that. I was teasing."

"And Dad," Blaise said, "here's your granddaughter Cora, who you haven't seen for awhile. Look how she's blossomed."

Cora blushed. She was sixteen, embarrassed by her enormous bosom that had taken her by surprise. Surprising her mother, too, who envied her daughter's mature breasts. Nora's chest was flat, by comparison. Cora wished her boobs would stop blossoming. Her father's remarks made her self-conscious. He'd purchased the dress for her to wear for the holidays, one he'd picked out, a dress more revealing than she was used to wearing.

Blaise added, "And here's your grandson, Logan, who you may or may not recognize with his shaved head and Mohawk, no less. He's gone punk. We hope it's a phase."

Logan, age seventeen, who wore black jeans, t-shirt, sneakers, and eyeliner, scowled at his father.

"Hi, Logan," said Birdie.

Logan nodded at his cousin. "Where's Flynn?"

"Upstairs," said Birdie. "In his room playing video games."

"So where's Sky?" Blaise glanced around the room. "Will she be gracing us with her presence?"

"She and Jess planned to stay here last night," said Iris. "Except their flight was cancelled, rescheduled for this morning. They should be arriving soon.

"Great," said Blaise. "I can't wait to listen to Sky talk non-stop about herself. I could use a drink. Ah, just the man. Hey, Bill."

Iris was relieved to have her husband join them. She thought of him as a gregarious teddy bear. She once told him he was so amiable he could most likely tame a nasty flu bug.

He walked across the room to shake Blaise's hand, gave Nora a light hug, then hugged Cora too. "Goodness," he exclaimed. "How you two kids have grown. He averted his eyes from Cora's cleavage. He paused at the sight of Logan before grabbing the boy in a bear hug, embarrassing him.

"Look at you, Logan. You're as tall as me, by the looks of it. What are you now?"

"Taller than you. Over six feet."

"Incredible." Bill clapped his hands. "Well, shall we get this party started?"

The expansive flagstone steps – a total of twenty-one, Sky knew, because she had once-upon-a-time counted them with her sister, Iris – led to a stoned entry archway. Boulders and greenery bordered the first nine steps, followed by a flat walking area, before ascending the remaining steeper twelve steps with iron handrails on both side.

"Hold up," said Sky, stopping to remove her light beige short ruched stiletto boots. She held her leather shoes and the strap of her matching purse, then walked in her stocking feet the remainder of the way. Jess and Sky pulled their respective suitcases, wheeling and yanking them up one, then the next, jagged stair to the landing under the archway. Jess reached the front door first. Sky was close behind and released the handle of her luggage.

"Jesus Christ," she said, wiping her forehead with the back of her hand. She stepped back into her boots. "I forgot how impractical this place is to get to."

Jess pulled out his iPhone, checking for messages as he waited for Sky to be ready. "We should have used the elevator at the back of the house."

"Unacceptable. That's no way to make an entrance. Can you believe this place was once a humble log cabin?"

"Hard to believe." Jess took a moment to admire the edifice while Sky caught her breath. "Sky, does coming here bring back fond memories for you?"

Sky wrinkled her nose at her husband as if he had farted.

Jess frowned. "What?"

"Nothing." Sky took hold of the luggage handle and rang the doorbell. "I'll concede. Before a certain time, we were all one big happy family. I had a fun, though bizarre, childhood."

Iris opened the door and screamed theatrically at seeing Sky.

Bill was at the ready to take Sky's bag.

"Come in! Come in!" Iris clutched her sister in a hug. "It's been too long. Gosh, don't you look like a star. I love your outfit, Sis."

Sky looked down at her own beige-on-beige layered clothing – short leather coat and skirt and green silk blouse – pleased with her choice of items. She'd decided on the attire after hours of indecision while Jess sat and waited, staring at his watch. Meanwhile, he had googled "indecisiveness" and saw the word was linked to behavior construed as neuroticism Their flight from LA hadn't been cancelled yesterday; they had missed their flight.

"You do look lovely," added Bill to his sister-in-law, kissing her on the cheek. "Jess, glad you made it. Can I take your luggage too? I'll roll both bags in the entry closet for now. Agreeable?"

"Fine by me. Unless you'd like to freshen up first. Sky?"

"What, Jess?" Her voice had a slight edge to it.

"Do you wish to freshen up, or go to our room first?"

"No. You go if you need to. I want to say hi to Dad."

※

Ashwood was staring at his grown children staring down at him paralyzed in his wheelchair. Sky, whom he hadn't seen in two years, and only twice after his stroke, leaned down and kissed him on the cheek. He felt nothing.

"Hi, Dad. Merry Christmas. I love you."

Parents were not supposed to have favorites but, as a child, Sky stood out as the brightest butterfly, fluttering around the house. Sky and Iris were fraternal twins, not identical. It was clear from the start that Sky had received the genetic exuberance of beauty, features that drew people to her. Iris was pretty too, but her gift was empathy – an attractive inner beauty. In many ways they complemented each other. In other areas, they did not. Ashwood recalled the adolescent tears whenever Iris was compared to Sky, feeling she had drawn the short straw from the genetic pool. Cassy engaged the twins in artistic activities to help them bond, to rely on one another, which helped, but Iris wasn't Sky, who had the boyfriends and was more popular. Sky knew she was prettier, but she never flaunted this fact, trying to include Iris in the higher social pecking order at school.

Ashwood watched as Sky, Iris, and Blaise began talking about him, as if he wasn't there. In a sense, he wasn't.

Jess went over to help Bill at the bar, mixing martinis. Ashwood had always been curious about Sky's husband who seemed aloof, not quite present, as if working on his next role and memorizing lines of dialog in his head. Self absorbed, as was Sky. When he did engage in conversation, he groused that strangers stopped him in the streets, at restaurants, at airports, recognizing his face but more than often not knowing his name, or getting it wrong. Nevertheless, he agreed to have his photo taken with them.

Upon relaying these episodes, his life as a movie star, Ashwood could tell it annoyed Sky. No one ever recognized her, only doing double takes to see if she was someone famous, even though she had appeared in popular TV series and pilots that never got picked up. She was the one asked by these strangers to take the photo.

Birdie listened and watched as her brother, Flynn, who was the same age as Cora, explain to his cousins the paranormal horror game called Phasmophobia that he was obsessed with. He talked them all into playing Friendly Fire since two or more players could participate in battling heavily armed androids. She walked out of his room, not interested in engaging in virtual warfare.

From the second floor, she took the spiral staircase down to the main level, which landed her in a long arched hallway. Essentially, it was an art gallery showcasing her Grandma Cassy's oil paintings. Her artwork could be found throughout the house, but this display was a retrospective of her early work, at the far end, to her later work, at the other end, leading into the living room.

Birdie frequently came to look at the art, wanting to understand the images. Her grandma's depictions of these men and women were so unusual. An exotic woman had hair turning into green tendrils and blossoming flowers. A businessman's head was a stormy cloud. A woman with four eyes and two mouths was playing chess with miniature men. As Birdie moved down the hall the paintings got even stranger. One painting showed a man's head submerged inside a porcelain toilet, revealing only his startled eyes, forehead, wet hair, and multiple colors spilling over the rim. Another showed the bust of a man whose face was covered with orange and yellow drips of paint. On the opposite wall was the face of a celebrity who Birdie couldn't name but recognized, whose head was melting below and exploding above like an aura or halo. The last canvas was thick and textured, entirely black, except for what she interpreted as red blood dripping from a tear at its center.

Birdie was puzzled by these last four paintings, searching for hidden messages. She walked into the living room where the adults were holding cocktails, standing in conversation, talking next to her grandfather in his wheelchair.

"Birdie!"

Her aunt leaned down to give her a hug, then stepped back to look at the red sweater with a white fuzzy reindeer. "You are so cute to wear that sweater. I love it."

Birdie glanced at her grandfather who shut his eyes, making her smile. She waved at Sky's husband, who waved back. Her brother had made fun of her for wearing the sweater, embarrassing her in front of their cousins who, in her mind, looked equally ridiculous – Cora wearing a dress that made her look like a high-priced hooker and Logan looking like he was auditioning for a slasher movie.

"Thanks, Sky. Dad bought it for me. Yes, I love it too."

The adults smiled and returned to the conversation they were having before being interrupted by Birdie's appearance.

"I can't get the image out of my mind." Jess was imagining his mother-in-law's story made into a movie. "That switchblade found with her decomposed body. Buried in the sand under tarps, an empty flask of vodka, and a camping shovel. It's inexplicable. Bizarre."

"That knife is the only item linking the murders." Sky took a sip from her martini and shuddered. "The other four victims were killed with a knife too. Could it have been the same one?"

Bill interjected, "The fatal wounds to the heart, in all four cases, matched. Remember, those detectives all suspected it might have been from a switchblade, but there was no DNA evidence."

Jess said, "That's because her remains weren't found until seven years after her disappearance. A fluke she was found at all. And why was she killed in Oregon? It makes no sense. The other victims died one after the other, a few months apart, in San Francisco."

Blaise gulped down some gin. "It's a mystery, that's for sure, that will likely never be solved."

Iris was exasperated with the conversation. "Why in heaven's name are we talking about Mother's murder on Christmas Day? This will only upset Dad." She glanced down at her father.

"Absolutely right, Dear," said Bill. "Bad form. Ah, look, the hors d'oeuvres have arrived. I'm famished. Shall we partake?"

As the adults moved toward the food, Birdie leaned down and whispered into her grandfather's ear. "Grandpa, I was looking at grandma's paintings again. The four at the end of the hallway, were they the last ones she painted before she died?"

Ashwood blinked four times.

"She was sending a message. I discovered a clue."

ASHWOOD

CHAPTER 6

1967

Cassy had strategized a plan. She knew it wasn't foolproof, because humans were fools. She easily hitched a ride to Highway 5, where she was dropped off, telling the elderly couple she would be meeting friends coming from Springfield to drive to Hendrick's Park. From there she walked to the freeway entrance going south and held out her thumb. Several cars stopped, but she waited for someone traveling to Ashland. She told the family of four she was visiting her father who worked for the Shakespeare Festival. He worked as a set designer for the company, she added, embellishing other lies about her fictitious father. At the freeway off ramp, she asked to be let out, because her dad would be picking her up there. The driver seemed puzzled, peering around at no buildings in sight. She thanked them, waving at this happy family who waved back, driving off.

This was easy, thought Cassy. Next, she planned to hitch a ride to Redding and tell the driver she was headed west to visit relatives on the coast in Eureka. In truth, she would find another ride going south into California, concocting a story about a school she'd be attending in Sacramento. If any of these people who had given her a ride happened to later notice a news bulletin about a missing girl matching her description, the police would only receive conflicting and false information about her possible whereabouts.

The next ride was in a semi truck. The driver was a man in his twenties, from what Cassy could discern. He was lanky, fairly good-looking, sporting a thin mustache that made Cassy smile to herself, imagining him as a cartoon character – a sly fox.

"Where you headed?"

"Redding." Cassy adjusted her backpack on her lap. "Thanks

for stopping. How far are you going?"

"Farther than that. Deep into California. Sure you don't want to go down there with me?"

"I'm sure. Relatives are waiting for me in Eureka."

"That's a drag."

"Why?"

"No reason. Making conversation."

"I'm not much of a talker."

"Me neither. I'm more a doer. A man of action." He grinned, looking more like a wolf. "You up for listening to some music?"

"Sure. I love all kinds."

"Bullshit. Gospel? Opera? Hillbilly tunes? You love that shit?"

"Not really."

"Got ya!" He cackled. "You can't bullshit a bullshitter. What's your angle anyway?"

"My what?"

"Why are you hitchhiking? How old are you?"

"Eighteen."

"Don't keep lying to me. Are you a runaway?"

"No."

He shook his head with a grin. "My name's Kyle. Apologies for not introducing myself properly."

"Brenda."

"It's a pleasure to make your acquaintance, Brenda. What is it ya do, Brenda?"

"What do you mean?"

"Everyone has to do something. Me, I race cars, ride dirt bikes, fuck around. Being a bad ass. That sort of thing. Your turn."

Cassy squirmed in her seat. "I like to draw."

"Draw? You mean like an artist?"

"Yeah." Cassy nervously opened her backpack. She pulled out her sketchbook. "See. I wasn't lying. I can draw you."

"Go ahead, do me. You're giving me chills already. I can't wait to see what you're capable of doing for me. Artistically."

Cassy held her breath to calm herself as she found one of her pencils. She shifted her body to lean against the door.

"It's best if you stay still and don't look at me."

"I can't promise you that, Brenda. But, what I want to know is, are you experienced?"

"What do you mean by that?"

Kyle inserted an 8-track cassette tape into a player unit mounted beneath the dashboard.

Cassy perked up, smiling. "Jimi Hendrix. I love this album."

"Right on." Kyle smiled at her and sang along to the lyrics.

"Purple haze all in my brain...

Lately things, they don't seem the same..."

After the first song, he pushed a button to fast forward the tape, stopping it a few times before finding the song he was searching for. He grinned at her as he tapped the steering wheel.

"You know you're a cute little heart-breaker, Foxy

And you know you're a sweet little love-maker, Foxy

I want to take you home, yeah

I won't do you no harm, no

You've got to be all mine, all mine

Ooh, foxy lady!"

Kyle slapped the steering wheel. "Great fucking song."

Cassy stayed focused on her drawing, but his mannerisms and the song's suggestive lyrics were unsettling.

She looked up and felt she had entered a time warp as the truck slowed down and pulled off the freeway. The expansive pavement had one building. She read the signs as they passed: "Men" over one door, and "Women" over another.

"Why are we stopping?"

Kyle said, "You ever hear of a rest stop?"

"I'm not tired," said Cassy. "If you need to use the restroom, why are we parking so far away?"

"For privacy. Time to see what talents you possess."

He grabbed the sketchpad out from her hands.

"Hey, I wasn't finished."

"I don't really give a shit." He looked at her drawing. "Not bad. Now, what other tricks can you do for me?"

"I don't know what you mean?"

"Compensation for me giving you a ride. Payment's come due."

"You can let me off here."

Cassy reached for the door handle. Kyle grabbed her wrist.

"Not so fast, stray cat."

"Let go of me!"

"I need to know if you're truly eighteen. Or if you've been lying about that too."

Cassy froze as he pulled her toward him. With his other hand, he spread open her leather jacket, lifted up her t-shirt, and cupped one breast, then felt the other.

"Sweet. Okay, Brenda, you passed the test."

Cassy tried to free herself but Kyle kept a tight grip to her wrist. He then opened a panel behind the seats to reveal a bed chamber.

"Now get up in there."

"No."

"I said, get the *fuck* inside! On that bed! Now!"

"No!"

He slapped her. "We can do this the fun way or the not-so-fun way. Either way, it's happening. Now move, Brenda!"

"I don't want to do this."

"That's not an option. Hey, what are you doing?"

With her free hand, Cassy reached into her backpack. "If you're determined to *fuck* me, Kyle, I want protection."

"Protection?"

"I have rubbers. I don't want to get pregnant."

"Fuck that. Skin to skin. That's the only way I—"

Kyle heard the metal click before Cassy lunged at him.

"Shit! Did you just—"

She retracted the switchblade before he could grab her hand.

"That was a warning! Let go of me! Let me out!"

"You fucking cunt!"

He held onto Cassy's arm as he pressed his other hand against his chest, trying to stem the bleeding.

"You're going to die for that!"

"No, I won't," said Cassy, steeling herself, waiting for him to glance down at his bleeding chest. She aimed for his heart next.

Cassy was shaking from the overload of adrenaline and shock of what she had done. She stood before the restroom sink, frantically washing blood off the knife and her hands, hoping no one would enter and see what she was doing. In the broken mirror, she looked as pale as a ghost. She slapped her face to bring back some color. Stuffing the knife back in her backpack, she exited the building.

She heard the motor of another semi truck nearby roar to life. She ran over, hopped onto the first step, then up to the next, taking hold of the side mirror to steady herself, and peered into the cabin. She tapped on the window.

The driver, a man in his forties, saw her smiling face waving at him from behind the pane of glass. He rolled down the window.

"Startled the life out of me, young lady. God-damned dangerous and foolish what you just did."

Cassy wondered what he had seen, trying not to panic.

"Hopping on my rig like that. What is it you want?"

"A ride. Please?"

"I'm a grouch. I like my solitude."

"Me too. I promise not to talk, unless you want me to."

"Where to?"

"California. Redding? If you're going that far."

"I am. Get in."

She opened the cab door and climbed inside. This rig was twice the size of the other one. The seats were new and luxurious.

"What kind of truck—"

The driver mimicked closing a zipper over his mouth.

Cassy nodded and kept quiet.

As the truck rolled onto the highway, she curled up like a cat on the spacious leather seat, resting her had against her backpack and closed her eyes, pretending to sleep.

Her runaway strategy had turned to shit. She had killed a man. But she had no choice. It was self-defense. No matter how much she rationalized her actions, she knew she had entered Hell. She began to cry, realized she was whimpering, remembering where she was, when she heard a man's voice.

"You okay? Did you need to talk?"

Cassy looked over at the driver, wiping away tears.

"No. Sorry. Bad dream."

"Go back to sleep. I'll let you know when we get to Redding. We'll be there in about an hour."

Her head returned to the pillow of her backpack. Cassy closed her eyes and willed herself to sleep, to be anywhere else. She wanted to be held, comforted by her mother's embrace, rubbing her back, telling her everything would be alright. But that bridge was burned. Now she could never go home, even if she wanted to turn back.

She was startled awake by a hand shaking her shoulder.

It was another time warp. The truck had stopped.

"Do you have a ride waiting? Someone meeting you?"

Cassy sat up, looking at the desolate vista. The sky was cloudy.

"What exit should I drop you off at?"

Cassy didn't know. She had never been outside Oregon. She had nowhere to sleep. No plan.

"You're driving to where in California?"

"Sacramento."

"My aunt and uncle live there. Can I stay and go there?"

"You're a strange bird. How old are you?"

"Eighteen."

"You don't look eighteen, but what the hell do I know."

"I start college near Sacramento this fall."

"UC Davis?"

"That's the one." Cassy straightened up in her seat.

"That's a good school. I'm Glen, by the way."

"Jenipher. Or, just Jen."

"Well, Jen, we'll be there in about two and a half hours."

"I'm going to major in art. And—"

Glen mimicked zipping his mouth shut.

Cassy nodded. "Do you mind if I draw you?"

"So long as you stay quiet."

Glen drove his rig back onto the freeway.

It was getting dark by the time they arrived in Sacramento.

Cassy looked around at the industrial area where they were stopped, the truck idling. She saw a restaurant across the street.

"Thank you for the ride, Glen."

"My pleasure."

"I just need to make a call. Is there a pay phone nearby?"

"That cafe should have one. Good luck at college."

"Thanks."

She exited the truck and walked over to the Blueberry Cafe.

Inside, she asked the cashier for the directions to a Greyhound bus station.

"You're in luck, darling. There's one about seven blocks from here. A good walking distance. Let me jot down the streets you need to take. I wouldn't want you going astray."

"Thanks."

Cassy was tired of hitching rides with strangers who she might have to kill. The memory of murdering a man made her shudder. She zipped up her leather jacket in defense against the cold weather and the dark of night closing in. Taking a bus to San Francisco was easy, and a better plan to avoid detection of her whereabouts. She would not be found, as long as Aaron or Victor didn't divulge her intent to be in the city where everything was happening. Where people came, wearing flowers in their hair, feeling free, getting high.

Cassy slept the night in the San Francisco bus terminal, nodding off on a seat in the waiting area until the morning light. She was instructed by a ticket agent which bus she needed to take to get to Golden Gate Park. By the time she arrived, it was still morning, the sky full of fog, and all the money she'd been able to squirrel away was gone, spent on bus fares. She walked into the massive park and became lost in wonder. She moved about aimlessly, until she noticed a few people wearing colorful outfits, their long hair streaming in a light breeze, all walking in the same direction.

Cassy followed after them, curious about their destination. She arrived with others into an expansive grassy field where a multitude of people had gathered. They were seated on blankets, dancing to flute music and drums. She stood, looking lost, until summoned by a man seated in a circle with others. He had a colorful headband around his long black hair, a multitude of beads hanging around his neck, and feathers tucked behind his ear. His buckskin jacket had fringe and his wide smile was directed up at her.

"Come join us." He patted the grass.

Cassy sat down. Two women were seated nearby. They were drawing flowers and hearts on each others faces.

"Who are you, beautiful creature?"

"Cassy."

"I'm Arrow."

"That's your real name?"

"It is now." He grinned and offered her a sugar cube.

"What do I do with that?"

Arrow placed the sugar in his mouth, murmuring as he reached into a leather satchel and removed another one, holding it out for her to take. "It makes the day sweeter and brighter."

Cassy plopped it in her mouth with a willing smile and instantly the sugar began to dissolve on her tongue. "I like your feathers. Oh, wait. I have some too." She removed her backpack, rumaged around at the bottom until she removed three crow feathers. She placed the black plumage in her hair.

"Welcome to our tribe. Just visiting?"

"No. Here to stay. Permanently. I arrived this morning."

"Groovy. Where from?"

"Far away."

"Do you have a place to crash?"

"Not yet."

"You do now. This is Melody and Harmony."

The two women turned to greet Cassy with smiles, giggling, then returned to face-painting each other.

"Come live with us."

"Where?"

"Our digs on Haight Street."

"As in Ashbury?"

"Yeah, Love Street. What do you say?"

She smiled. "Okay." Her arrival felt surreal.

The sugar cube began to melt inside Cassy's brain. In time, she saw the meadow rising and the people sparkling with new colors.

CHAPTER 7

1974

A degree in architecture was a five-year program, and Aaron had no intention of staying in college for one year longer than he had to, having been disillusioned with his life goals after Cassy ran away. He graduated with a degree in journalism with no clue what he would do with the certificate. The war in Vietnam was still producing body bags being sent home. His high number in the lottery drawing left him free of worry of being drafted into any military service where he would be trained to kill people he didn't know.

After hustling around, giving interviews, he found employment as a freelance photographer for an advertising agency, and part-time work building set designs for a theater company in San Francisco. He was paying rent to live within the side of a hill on Summit Drive in Corte Madera. It had been a garage, converted into a rental unit by the owner of a mansion who lived above with a swimming pool and a panoramic vista. Aaron described his living space as a hobbit hole with a view of the bay.

On assignment to photograph an acute rehabilitation center for pictures to be used in a brochure, Aaron walked with the person in charge of the project throughout the hospital. The facility specialized in treating patients with spinal cord and brain injuries, as well as stroke and burn victims. It bothered Aaron to be taking photos of these disabled people who were suffering. He had permission to shoot them, yet he felt guilty, as if invading their privacy. He hid behind the lens of his camera, clicking off shots of paralyzed victims receiving therapy in swimming pools and learning to walk, talk, and perform the rudimentary tasks of a child. In one room, a circle of brain-damaged patients, all in wheelchairs, were tossing a beach ball to one another as a means to regain nerve and muscle mobility.

One of the wheelchair patients kept reaching toward him. The man appeared to be in his late twenties, but it was hard to tell. His jaw was slack and his lips protruded as he uttered urgent-sounding, emotionally-charged words that Aaron couldn't understand. Aaron smiled back to be friendly but he was there to do a job, not engage with the patients.

He asked one of the nurses about the man's condition, curious to know the cause of his injury. It was a freak accident that ocurred during the summer, from falling off a ski lift while working to repair the equipment. His head struck the base of the cement foundation. She told Aaron other sad stories. Another one of her patients, during his early-morning commute to the city from Sonoma, had struck a runaway horse that ran onto the freeway. Its entire body went through the windshield, causing brain damage to the driver.

Later that day, Aaron was asked to take photos of the bedroom facilities. Alone in one of the rooms, he browsed around, picking up an array of framed photos. One picture showed a muscular man, tanned and shirtless, with a beautiful woman seated on his lap. They both had laughing smiles, full of love for each other. The next framed picture revealed a photo of the man who'd reached out to him, trying to tell him something but was unable to articulate his thoughts.

The slow realization that these two men were the same person, before and after photos, shook Aaron to the core. The second photo showed this damaged man seated in his wheelchair, beside a young woman crouched next to him. Her sweet adoring smile was strained, clearly struggling emotionally to look happy.

It was Cassy!

The man in the rehab facility was her older brother, Victor.

He set both framed photos back on the nightstand. He felt the room begin to spin. Victor was disabled, no longer the same person he once was. Yet he recognized Aaron as someone he knew in the past. Aaron recalled Victor from seven years ago – the confident, kind-hearted brother. It gutted Aaron with sadness, trying to process the pain, imagining Victor's brain in pieces, like shards of glass.

His emotions were conflicted, because he felt elation too, now realizing Cassy was alive. She was, most likely, living somewhere in San Francisco. Aaron talked to the hospital staff and explained his connection to the patient and his sister, enquiring about an address for Cassy, or a phone number. He was told they were not permitted to release that information to non-family members.

Weeks passed with no luck locating Cassy. He checked all the bay area phone books but there was no listing for a Cassy Crow or Cassandra Crow. Of course, she wouldn't publish her phone number even if she had one. Since his college days, Aaron had a picture frame with two photos of Cassy. The ones he took at the beach – her funny distorted face on one side and, on the other, her solemn expression with penetrating eyes.

He kept staring at her photos, obsessed again, wanting to find her. He put the picture frame back on his desk. He was in his rented office space near the San Francisco Embarcadero where he kept his design and photo equipment. He was waiting for Gina to arrive. She was driving into the city from the east bay. She was the ex-girlfriend of his best friend whom she dumped after discovering he'd slept with Aaron's girlfriend. This happened a month before they'd graduated from high school. During their teenage years, he'd never imagined they'd end up together. Gina and his best friend had been a couple for five years, and thus unattainable. As close friends, they went on double-dates to the movies and trips to the beach. Aaron's girlfriends changed from year to year. Their tight-knit group would sneak out of their houses in the middle of the night, meet on a golf course, and slide down the groomed slopes on blocks of ice – one of the acts of mischief they instigated as a means of rebellious fun.

Aaron heard the door buzzer and went to let Gina inside.

He laughed at the sight of her. She was dressed in a frayed white gown with bandages covering her body, her face painted white with black lips, and a conical hairdo with lightning streaks

"You look ghastly. Shockingly beautiful, disguised as you are. Who, exactly, are you?"

"Can't you tell? The Bride of Frankenstein."

"I could've dressed as the monster, if you'd let me know."

"It figured you'd dress up as a wizard."

"Because of my special powers?"

"No, because silver moons and stars on your purple dunce cap suits you. The black robe is a nice touch. Adds some credibility. Grab your magic wand, give me a kiss, and let's go. We'll be late."

They were attending a first-of-its-kind event. It was being called the Hooker's Ball. A masquerade party organized by COYOTE (Call Off Your Old Tired Ethics), providing legal help for prostitutes. Aaron was friends with one of the organizers, who worked at the theater company, and encouraged them to attend.

The venue was dark, crowded, and noisy, swarming with wildly imaginative costumes. Gina and Aaron wandered about enjoying the display of freakish characters – a businessman wearing a suit made of money, a swashbuckling pirate, a fire-breathing dragon, a group of naked women in body paint wearing only long tails. They stopped at the sight of a tall woman dressed in white, an angel with a chain around her neck. She was being pulled along by a small hunched, sinister-looking man, dressed in black.

From the other direction approached a towering man with bolts in his neck and head, dressed as Frankenstein's monster.

"Look, your husband came," joked Aaron.

As the Bride and Monster crossed paths, they acknowledged one another with a nod, then moved along.

On their search to find a bar serving alcohol, Aaron and Gina were stopped by the sight of something coming at them. A bird with black-feathered wings – startling Aaron as it flew and leapt onto his body, grasping hold with its arms and legs.

"I found you!"

Cassy held onto Aaron, wildly kissing him.

Gina was amused and then confused when the woman remained attached to Aaron, not letting go. "What's going on?"

Cassy dropped to her feet. "I'm Cassy. I'm sure you're lovely. But Aaron is mine. I found him first."

"Aaron?"

"Gina," said Aaron, "this is Cassy."

"Yes, I heard."

"She disappeared seven years ago."

"I ran away."

Dressed as a crow in a black cape of feathers, Cassy spread her wings around Aaron. "I like that you're a wizard. And your hair is longer too. I can't believe we'll be together again."

Aaron held Cassy, looking sheepishly at Gina, who was clearly annoyed.

"Is she the one in those photos you keep on your desk?"

"You have photos of me?"

"Aaron has photos of me, too," said Gina. "We're together. I'm his girlfriend. We're planning on getting married."

This was news to Aaron, caught off-guard by her remark.

"Which explains your wedding dress," said Cassy. "It's lovely. But you can't marry him. He's going to marry me."

Gina glowered at Aaron.

The noise in the hall was deafening.

"Listen," said Aaron, "I can barely hear myself think in here. Why don't we find the bar and get some drinks so we can all talk and hear ourselves?"

"Not until you tell me what the hell she's talking about?"

"Gina," said Aaron. "What about you? We've never once talked about getting married."

"It was understood. We've been dating for three years!"

"I'm sure Aaron loves you," said Cassy. "But not in the way he loves me. We realized we're soul mates. Tell her, Aaron."

Gina scowled. "Yes, *tell* me, Aaron."

Cassy stood beside Aaron, taking hold of his hand, rubbing his palm with her thumb. "Are we still in love?"

He looked at Cassy. "You ran away."

"I had to. But I always knew you'd find me."

"I was trying to find you."

"We found each other. It's magic."

"Give me your keys."

Aaron's attention returned to Gina. She held out her hand. He hesitated, then reached inside his wizard's cape to find his pockets, and placed his car keys in her palm.

"I'm taking your car. Driving to your studio to get mine. Then I'm driving home. If you come to your senses, call me. I love you, Aaron. And I thought you loved me too."

"I do, Gina."

"But she has some kind of power over you, and I'm not sure I can compete with that."

After Gina left, so too did Aaron and Cassy. They walked a few blocks to a cafe, bought wine at the bar, and found a table by the window. Since it was Halloween, other people were in costumes, yet they stood out, dressed as a crow and wizard drinking wine.

Once seated, they simply stared at one another without saying a word. Aaron had become mesmerized again by Cassy's green irises, staring back, surrounded by her aura of black feathers.

"Do you have a boyfriend?"

"Do I look like the sort of person who has boyfriends?"

Aaron laughed, reminded of the same remark, coming from an assertive, fifteen-year-old girl when they'd first met.

"Does that mean you're still a virgin?"

Cassy smiled, sipping her wine. "Did you want me to be?"

"You should know, I'm incapable of doing real magic." Aaron held up his hand, extending all five digits, then doing the same with his other hand, stopping after two fingers as he mentally calculated. "Ah, you're twenty-two years old."

"It must be your college education. I'm now legally able to drink alcohol. And legally allowed to do other things and not get people locked in jail. Are you building mansions and skyscrapers yet?"

"I'm not an architect. I dropped out of the program."

"To do what?"

"Well, to date, I work for a theater company, helping to design and build stage sets."

"That's impressive," said Cassy.

"Hardly. But I like it. That's where I copped this outfit."

"Wait. You're not a real wizard?"

"I also get hired, occasionally, to shoot photos for an ad agency. Projects come and go. I freelance. What about you?"

"I freeload. At least, I did when I first arrived here. I stayed in a few communal homes in the Haight. One Victorian housed members of a band. I helped cook meals and clean the rooms. Which was a pigsty with free drugs. In return, I didn't starve and had a place to sleep. Do you want to hear something funny?"

"Sure. Humor me."

"On my first day in San Francisco, I went to Golden Gate Park. There was some kind of Be-In happening. The first person I met was a man who greeted me with a smile and a sugar cube. I had no idea what he was offering."

"I can guess: LSD."

"That was some first day. It flipped me out royally."

Aaron nodded. "I've had my share of acid and mescaline trips. I stopped taking psychedelics after I nearly flunked out of college."

"Same here. Except for the college drop-out part. Been there, done that. No more tripping for me."

"Do you still draw?"

"I mainly paint now. I share an art studio with four guys. We call ourselves the Gang of Five. Do you want to see our place?"

"Sure. Now?"

"Yes, now. I live there too. It's a warehouse we rent in SoMa." She gulped down the remainder of her wine. "It's not that far, within walking distance. Unless you want to take a cab."

"Or I could magically transport us there. Can you fly?"

"I say we walk."

"I thought you said it wasn't far."

"I lied." Cassy held Aaron's hand. "I wanted to walk with you. And it's within walking distance. See, we're almost there."

She pointed to a four-story, brick industrial building that looked as if it could be abandoned.

"This is not a great section of town."

"It's what we can afford. It's spacious. You'll love it."

Aaron hated it. The entrance had a sliding metal door. Inside the cement-floor entryway were several motorcycles parked in a corner. The metal staircase reverberated, bouncing off the brick walls that led to the second level. The room was an enormous open space that had cement columns and a tall ceiling with metal beams. Near the center of the room was an arrangement of furniture. People could be seen seated and standing. Aaron's first impression of this cluster was an island formed of flotsam, gathered within a sea of easels, paint cans, wood crates, a row of porcelain toilets, coils of wire, and a set of drums. Against the white-washed walls were stacks of canvases, oil paintings, and three-dimensional art objects hung, some framed, some not, works in progress.

As Cassy and Aaron approached, they were greeted by a jovial voice, "Look who's come home to roost! What is that you brought back with you, wayward crow?"

"That would be a *man*, Jimmy. A sorcerer. So play nice. Or he will transform you into a rodent."

"I know how to behave myself. I'm a Brit. We have manners."

Aaron was bemused by the appearance of this Jimmy, sprawled upon a paint-stained couch, unmoving, except to raise a glass with amber liquid in a pseudo toast. He wore red bell-bottom jeans, green alligator boots, and a tacky tropical shirt beneath a leather jacket, looking self-assured for someone dressed so ridiculously, and whose head looked reduced in scale by his large golden afro.

"Welcome to our oasis, a land of enchantment where dreams are born. Introductions, Cassy, are in order."

"This is Aaron. And these, Aaron, are my lovely flatmates."

In one chair sat a large bearded man wearing overalls, who was barefoot, holding a beer can and a smile. On a zebra-striped sofa sat a bare-chested man wearing leather pants who looked like a fashion model, unsmiling, but welcoming with a nod. Atop his head was a gold crown, and on his lap sat an equally fashionable woman who appeared to be wearing only a robe. Nearby stood a man dressed in white corduroys, t-shirt, and sneakers, dipping brushes into paint cans and flicking streaks of color onto a canvas spread out upon the floor. He turned to acknowledge the visitor, raising his eyebrows, as if to say hello. A smoking cigarette hung from his lips.

Cassy spread her wingspan of feathers to gesture at the room and all the walls. "Well, this is it. My workspace and living quarters. Why aren't you guys out riding your motorcycles, creating havoc, or wearing costumes at some party, tricking-and-treating?"

"We're serious artists," said the bearded man. "Unlike you, we have no time to be flighty and flit around town partying when there is important work to be done."

Cassy laughed and flipped him off. "Oscar, you know shit. And who's the better artist among us?"

"That would be me," said the man wearing a crown.

"That's Luca," said Cassy. "He's famous for assembling junk to canvases constructed from wood pallets. Recyclable art. He thinks what he does makes him the new Michaelangelo."

Luca said, "Who?"

"He recently finished another masterpiece." Cassy pointed to a pyramid of stacked painted porcelain. "It's a series of toilets."

"We should all honor the humble toilet," said Luca. "It's one of mankind's greatest achievements. Pure genius."

"Hi, Liz." Cassy waved to the robed woman. "Lizzy is a live-in friend and our favorite groupie."

"Artists have groupies?" said Aaron

"I'm a professional ornament," said Liz. "I model for Luca."

"Who can't even draw," dissed Cassy playfully.

"I can *draw*," Luca countered. "I choose to be discreet with my abilities. Only applied when it requires my crowning touch."

"You prima donna. Go sit on your throne. I'm going upstairs." Cassy grabbed Aaron's hand and pulled him along, passing the man flicking paint. "How's it coming, Parker?"

"I have no clue. Inspiration will come to me eventually."

"Splatter on."

Stopping below another flight of stairs, Cassy turned to point and say, "My stuff is over in that far corner of the room."

"I want to see your art."

"You will. But first you must experience my *boudoir*."

Cassy's makeshift room consisted of a space within a corner of the four walls where two curtains of fabric hung from the ceiling that created two walls. She entered through the opening of the tent-like structure to reveal her bedroom.

"Ta-da! Isn't it cozy?"

Surrounded by an array of small oriental rugs was a queen-size mattress on the floor with a quilted bedspread and colorful pillows. Next to the bed was a standing mirror, a wardrobe, a lamp, a chair, a chest of drawers, a nightstand, a space heater, a microwave oven, a coffee maker, and a mini refrigerator.

On the painted-white brick walls hung two oil paintings.

"Do you like my place?"

"Umm, yeah. So this is you," said Aaron

"This is me. I don't require much. As you can see."

"Where's the bathroom?"

"Back down there. In the hall. It's communal."

"You live like a gypsy."

"I *am* a gypsy. Time to take off my feathers."

Aaron removed his hat and cloak as Cassy removed her cape of black plumage, along with her beret with crow feathers, tossing both items onto the chair. She was left wearing a long-sleeve black turtleneck and tights, along with boots she unlaced, and tossed off too. She looked up to find Aaron standing and staring at the wall.

"Is that supposed to be me?"

Cassy glanced at the painting above her bed. "It is you. I painted it from memory. And from that drawing I did. Remember? And that one," she pointed to the other wall, "is a portrait of Victor."

"These paintings are amazing, but—" Aaron stopped. His voice triggered a mood shift into a somber tone.

"What?"

"I know about Victor."

"How?"

"I was there."

"Where?"

"At the rehab center. I was hired to photograph the facility for a brochure. He was in a wheelchair and he, I don't know, recognized me. He reached out, touching me, trying to say something."

"Oh, God." Cassy welled up with tears. She came over and held onto Aaron. "It's so horrible!"

"I didn't realize it was Victor. Not until I saw the photos in his room. The before and after ones. And the one with you. That's when I realized you were likely here in the city. I tried to find you."

"Aaron, I don't know what to do. My life is a mess. I feel so lost and helpless and *stupid*. Victor needs my help. And I need your help. Please, Aaron, help me."

"Tell me what I can do."

Cassy removed a bottle of chardonnay from her refrigerator. She poured wine into two thrift-shop vintage glasses. Along her dresser she had several small crystal receptacles whose colors and styles were all different. Sitting on her mattress, Cassy told Aaron about her father who had died after an operation to remove a second brain tumor. Her mother became sick from grief. She couldn't cope with the multiple tragedies – a teenage daughter who had run away from home, a husband whose personality turned toxic resulting from cancerous growths, and a son who fell in a freak accident leaving him brain damaged and disabled.

After six years, Cassy had ventured home to visit her family and discovered the fate of her father and brother. She'd reconciled with her mother, asking forgiveness for running away. Once forgiven and told she was still loved, Cassy found her mother dead one morning, having overdosed on sleeping pills.

Aaron was stunned, processing her loss. Cassy had inherited a modest sum of money from selling her parents' house in Oregon. She sold the furniture and contents. There was a small savings account, which amounted to very little after state and federal taxes were deducted. What money remained was spent on hospital fees, but not enough to cover the ongoing costs. Hospital representatives advised her to hire an attorney to file a lawsuit against the ski resort. Victor's accident had occurred during the summer while he was working on a ski lift, doing repairs atop one of its towers, when an employee engaged the power by mistake, causing him to fall.

"That's negligence," said Aaron. "The ski resort is totally liable. I know an attorney who handles personal injury claims. This is good. I mean, you know what I mean. It's bad. But you and Victor stand to receive a huge financial judgement. It'll help pay for his medical bills and home care."

"Do you really think so?"

"I'm almost certain. I'll make a call tomorrow."

"Thank you, thank you." She hugged Aaron and reached for the bottle of wine. "I need this." She filled their glasses. "Also this." She leaned over to open a drawer beside her bed and removed a small glass pipe and butane lighter. She flicked the spark wheel, producing a flame, igniting the bowl, inhaling deeply, and handing the smoking pipe over to Aaron.

"What is it?"

Cassy exhaled a plume of smoke. "Hash."

Aaron took a puff and handed it back to Cassy who then set it in an ashtray. "I need to tell you something."

"Okay."

"I haven't told anyone else." Cassy paused to breathe and rake fingers through her hair. "I killed a man."

"You … what?"

"With Victor's knife. It was self-defense."

"When? How did—"

"Seven years ago. While I was hitchhiking to get here. A truck driver tried to rape me."

"*Jesus*, Cassy."

"I know. But Jesus wasn't there to save me. This fucking perv threatened to kill me. I acted fast, and stabbed him in the heart."

"Are you sure he died?"

"He's dead. I have blood on my hands. It haunts me."

Aaron imagined a nuclear explosion clouding his head from her confession, her family tragedies, the alcohol, the hash. "Shit."

"I know. My life is shit."

Aaron snapped back. "*No*. You had no choice. You did what you had to do to survive, right?"

"That's right."

"You can't blame yourself."

"I do."

"Don't. Come here." He pulled Cassy into an embrace.

"Does that mean you still love me?"

"Always. Unequivocally."

"Good. Then fuck me, please."

Aaron pulled away with a grin, looking her in the eyes. "Don't you mean make love to you?"

She kissed him. "That's what I meant."

※

They were snuggling under the covers of her bed.

"You're a great lover too," said Cassy. "I knew you would be. It felt perfect when we kissed the first time."

"You're amazing too."

Cassy pulled down the bedsheets. "Like my amazing breasts? They're kinda small."

"I love your breasts. They're perfect handfuls."

"Kiss them again, please."

Aaron kissed both nipples. "Can I ask you something?"

"Depends."

"I'm curious about your situation here."

"Explain."

"It's none of my business, but…"

"But?"

"Are you in a relationship with any of these guys?"

Cassy laughed. "God, no. We're just friends." She took hold of his genitals. "This is to reassure you. From this time forward, only you have access to me. And I to you. *Yours* is now mine."

Aaron grinned back. "Understood. Agreed."

"Good. Those are the rules." She let go of him and sat up in bed against the array of pillows. "I'm no prude. I've had sex with other men. I've slept around some, but not like a whore."

"Since we're being honest, so have I."

"Had sex with men?"

"I meant with women. Double standards about sex, regarding men versus women, that sort of thing. But I'm curious, how did you happen to meet your flatmates?"

"Through Oscar. He was living in the Haight house too. He was the drummer in the band. They called themselves the Gang of Five.

I had an affair with the guitar player, Eric. I went on tour with them. At first, it was exciting. The road trips. The crappy motels. Then it got shitty. Sometimes dangerous, but Oscar was there to protect me, and we became buddies. I caught Eric getting blow jobs back stage and fucking groupies in cars and vans. It became too much. We fought. The band broke up midway through the tour, and Oscar and I found our way back to San Francisco by taking a bus."

"You've only mentioned having sex with one guy."

"I fucked around to get even. As if that was any help. Speaking of double standards, Eric got furious that I was screwing other men. He hit me, and that was it. I talked Oscar into leaving the Haight house with me. Besides being a drummer, Oscar wanted to pursue painting. Luca and Parker are guys he knew from a motorcycle club. Jimmy came over from swinging London and met Luca at some art class. They all ride choppers. That's how we came together."

"To be the Gang of Five?"

"We stole the name from the band that broke up."

"Do you get along with all of them?"

"They're harmless and fun. Truth be told, I'm the only one who knows how to draw. Oscar is a devotee of Rothko. He applies layers of paint, creating textures and geometric patterns. Interesting colors, but I'm fascinated by the human figure. Parker idealizes Pollock and flicks and drips paint to create abstractions. Luca, he was smitten by Duchamp's conceptual art. He considers Fountain a masterpiece."

"What's that?"

"The display of a urinal, presented as art. It changed the history of art forever. For the worse, in my opinion. Luca can actually draw but uses this ability sparingly."

"Is he the one you called a prima donna?"

"We tease each other a lot. It's all in good fun."

"And Jimmy?"

"*He* is the prima donna. Too full of himself. But a riot."

"He looks kinda wild."

"He is. With a wicked sense of humor."

"And his art?"

"Celebrity faces. He's obsessed with famous people. Replicating them to death. I call him Andy War*hole*. Or just *Ho*."

"What do they call you?"

Cassy laughed. "'Flight Risk.' 'Little Bitch.' Pet names like that. I was still in my teens when we moved into this art studio. They're all in their twenties, pushing thirty."

"My guess is they're jealous of your talent."

"Thanks. But it's true. I *can* be a bitch. Now roll over and fuck me good and hard like you really mean it."

Aaron laughed.

"What I meant was, please love me?"

"Maybe they resent the fact you don't mince words."

Cassy and Aaron were lying in bed post-coital, happily satiated and fulfilled. Cassy announced, "I need to pee badly."

She threw back the sheets, stood, hesitating to cover herself.

"No time." She ran through the opening in the fabric walls into the open space, shouting, "Stay clear! Naked woman running!"

Aaron sat up in bed, amused and perplexed by this enigma of a woman he loved. He wondered what his parents would think when he introduced them to her and, in turn, how she'd be meeting them. Now that they were intrinsically coupled, he wondered about their future. He lay there musing, recalling their trip to the ocean, when she'd leapt onto his body as if she were a playful, inquisitive octopus wrapping its tentacles lovingly around him and not letting go.

Aaron smiled, realizing he'd been, and was, hooked.

ASHWOOD

CHAPTER 8

2020

Blaise was staring out the front window, sipping his martini, when he noticed movement in the garden, near the fountain. It was a young black boy prowling around. Wearing khakis, a dress shirt, and a sports jacket, he didn't appear to be dressed like someone who was there to rob the place. He moved about suspiciously, though, eyeing this and that, scrutinizing the house, before venturing up the steps toward the front door.

Blaise acted fast to confront this intruder, opening the door and finding the boy about to ring the buzzer.

"Is there something I can help you with? We don't allow any solicitations. This is Christmas, for God's sake."

The boy dropped his hand. "I wasn't soliciting."

"Then why were you snooping around?"

"I wasn't snooping, Sir."

"No? I clearly saw you looking—"

"Birdie invited me."

Blaise frowned, trying to assimilate the notion of his niece tied in some way with this boy.

Bill noticed activity happening at the front door and approached his brother-in-law and the young man at a standstill.

"Are you Drake?"

"Yes, Sir."

"Welcome. Come in. You're Birdie's friend, yes?"

"I am. Thank you."

Blaise moved aside, observing the boy as he entered, seeing him as a potential interloper with ulterior motives.

As the adults hovered around to greet him, shaking hands and asking questions, Drake looked around for Birdie who was nowhere in sight.

"We met at school," said Drake, stammering. "Well, actually, I mean, it wasn't at Willow Creek Academy where she goes to classes, because I, you see, attend Tamalpais High—"

"We met during a field trip," interrupted Birdie, coming up to stand beside him, addressing the adults.

Drake glanced at her with relief. "Hi. That's right."

"Remember, Mom, when our class went on that field trip into San Francisco to visit the museum?"

"Vaguely, I think," said Iris. "You mean, the DeYoung?"

"That's the one," said Drake. "Several schools were visiting the museum that day. That's when I met your daughter."

Birdie smiled at the adults who were looking down with drinks in hand, attempting to follow the threads of their explanations as to how and why they knew each other.

"I saw Drake staring at Grandma Cassy's painting. At the one she's probably the most famous for. The one called '*Jesus Wept.*'"

"It's stunning," said Drake.

"Yes, it is," said Iris. "But how—"

"Did we become friends?" Birdie glanced at Drake to make sure they were following the rehearsed script. "Because I asked him if he liked her paintings."

"Which, of course, I do."

"And it turns out he's a fan of her work."

"I created a blog that's all about Cassandra Crow."

"I told him I was her granddaughter."

Sky asked Drake pointedly, "What *kind* of blog?"

"Oh, right," he said. "Well, mainly, it's a celebration of her art, giving my interpretations of each piece. What I believe she's saying, and how much her work means to me. That sort of thing."

Birdie interjected, "He's also trying to solve her murder."

"Excuse me?" said Iris.

"I'm an amateur sleuth." He smiled nervously.

"Ah-ha!" said Blaise, pleased with himself. "There it is. I sensed something shady about you."

"There's nothing shady about me. Really."

"Uncle Blaise," said Birdie, "Drake and I became friends from our chance meeting. I invited him so he could see more of Grandma's art and show him her studio where she worked."

"On Christmas?" Blaise sensed something was amiss. "Doesn't your own family have—"

"We celebrate Kwanzaa. Actually, not much of anything."

"Blaise," chastised Iris, "stop grilling the boy. He's been invited to join us for Christmas. And for dinner. Enough said."

"We're happy to have you," said Bill. "Any friend of Birdie's is welcome in our home. You two go have some fun. There's plenty to experience in this extravagant house. Artwork everywhere."

Birdie and Drake walked away. Her voice, as she whispered, had a tinge of sarcasm, "Well *that* went great, I thought."

"I hate lying," said Drake.

"It wasn't a lie. We have become friends."

"I know. But we met online, not at some museum."

"So?"

Ashwood watched as the two of them approached.

"Grandpa, this is my friend, Drake. He's a big fan of Grandma's paintings. Do you mind if I show him her art?"

Ashwood closed his eyes.

"That means no. Is it okay if I show Drake her studio too?"

Ashwood blinked.

"When he blinks, that means yes."

Drake felt ill at ease in front of her grandfather, whose eyes were focused on him, and the only part of him that moved. He looked to Birdie for help. "What do I say?"

"It has to be a 'yes' or a 'no' question."

"Hi. Birdie and I are friends. Is that okay with you?"

Ashwood blinked.

"See?" said Birdie. "He likes you. I love you, Grandpa."

Birdie took hold of Drake's hand and directed him toward the other side of the room. "I'll give you a tour of the house."

"What happened to your grandfather?"

"He had a massive stroke," said Birdie. "It makes me sad. He designed and constructed this entire place. It was what Grandpa and Grandma called their love nest, and named our house the Crowsnest, for creating art and giving life to everyone in it."

"Does that include me?"

Birdie laughed. "Possibly." She squeezed his hand, and then pushed a button on a pedestal. "Watch what this does." The sliding glass doors opened.

"Cool," said Drake.

They walked out onto the deck where there was a massive bar with a shiny wood top and a matching table. There was also a stone fire pit and a built-in barbecue within a rock wall.

"Wow," said Drake. "Super cool area."

"I know, right?" Birdie was happy showing off their house. "Wait until you see Grandma Cassy's art studio. It's over there. See? Across that bridge."

"What's in that cottage over there?"

"That's where Grandpa lives. He built it for Grandma Cassy's brother. He was disabled in a ski accident. There's a separate room for a live-in nurse who takes care of Grandpa. She's on holiday with her family. A temporary nurse is coming this afternoon. I'm the one helping Grandpa until she arrives."

Birdie walked off the deck onto one of the three bridges with Drake following. She pointed at various things on the property – the brook and pond, a hammock stretched between two redwood trees, sporadic sculptures of angels hiding within the garden and stationed like guardians on the porch of the art studio.

Birdie removed a key that was hidden beneath a wood carving of a crow and unlocked the door.

The wood structure had a tall ceiling and multiple shelves with stored canvases. There were three standing easels, one holding an unfinished painting. Tables had brushes sticking out of ceramic jars, paint tubes in glass fishbowls, and stacks of paint cans. The wood flooring had paint stains. Two walls without shelving were painted white. At the center of the walls were rectangular spaces untouched by paint where canvases had been hung for large pieces. Surrounding these blank areas were explosions of color. One wall was splattered in red paint. It looked like the aftermath of a crime scene.

Drake was in awe, taking it all in, imaging Cassy at work. After a silent minute, he spoke. "People said she went mad."

"I know," said Birdie. "But she was sweet."

"Was she ever violent?"

"Never. Her explosive imagination came out in her paintings. She was a tortured artist, Mom said."

"Maybe caused by artists being murdered?"

Birdie swiped at a tear. "Her breakdown happened before those murders started. Mom said she was my age when she noticed her behavior change. No one knows what happened. Not even Grandpa. But something horrible happened. It remains a mystery."

"I did research on the other painters. The ones she'd lived with when she was younger. The four who were killed."

"They called themselves the Gang of Five. Weird, huh?"

"Why do you think they were all killed? And your grandmother being the last one? What was the motive?"

Birdie wiped away another tear. "She didn't deserve to die. Not like that. Mom said she was strange, but funny and kind."

"I'm puzzled by the switchblade found beside her remains."

Birdie twitched as if touched by a ghost.

Drake said, "You okay? We don't have to talk about this."

"It's okay. Let me show you what I discovered."

They were staring at the paintings in the hallway. Birdie pointed to the face she sort of recognized, whose features were melting below and exploding above.

"I know who that is," said Drake. "Don't you?"

"No," said Birdie.

"Andy Warhol, I think. He was an artist too. He got famous for doing a lot of pop art. Series and reproductions of celebrities. That was one of his phases. There's a similarity in style here, at its center, but combined with Cassy's, Cassandra's, sorry – I mean, your grandmother's style of painting."

"You can call her Cassy. She'd like that."

"This is representative of her later artwork."

"It was one of her last paintings. Grandpa confirmed it."

"But the face has, like, a double exposure. See?" Drake pointed at the lines of color around his eyes and cheeks. "And, Birdie, you know what?"

"What?"

"I found photos of the other four painters she lived and worked with. One of the guys was named Jimmy. I think that's who this other face is supposed to be."

"Holy shit," said Birdie. "That's another clue."

"What do you mean?"

"Look there. By her signature. There's one vertical stroke."

"So?"

Birdie moved to the next painting. See there? Two strokes."

"Another guy she lived with created a series of painted toilets, and other art objects. He was the second murder victim. This has to be about him. She painted his head in a toilet bowl."

Birdie pointed to the next painting. It was the portrait of a man with a face composed of splatters and drips of paint."

"Like a Jackson Pollock."

"Who?"

"The artist who dripped paint on canvases. He was famous for that technique. Like here, over his face, combined with Cassy's style. He was the third artist killed, and an imitator of Pollock."

"There." said Birdie. "See, it has three vertical strokes."

"Okay. Weird. His name was Parker."

"Look at this last painting," said Birdie. "It's completely black, thick and textured. Except for what looks like blood oozing from a hole in its center. Like a stab wound?"

"Wow," said Drake."And four vertical marks by her signature. He was the fourth victim in the serial killings. All this has to mean something."

"I know," said Birdie. "They're clues. But to what?"

"Do you know which painting was her last?"

"Come with me."

Birdie and Drake were both standing on their tiptoes, peering at the large painting above the fireplace.

Blaise noticed and walked over munching on an appetizer.

"What are you two up to now?"

"Hi, Uncle Blaise. You're taller than us."

"That's true."

"Can you see if there's anything next to Grandma's signature on this painting? Along the bottom. We can't tell from here."

Blaise stepped onto the hearth extension to get a closer look.

"Okay. Next to her signature there appears to be tally marks. Four vertical lines and one diagonal crossed through. Like a number. The number five. I have no idea what that signifies. A date?"

Birdie and Drake looked at one another as if they'd been given the key to unlock a secret door.

"Do you know what it means?"

Birdie nodded. "Not sure. We think we might."

CHAPTER 9

1977

Cassy was enjoying her unofficial going away party. With a glass of wine in hand, she glanced around at the crowd of people gathered in their art studio, wandering about, checking out all the artwork on display. For this occasion, she wore a gypsy patchwork floral lace trim tiered skirt and a short black t-shirt top. Across the room, Oscar was working the sound system, playing tapes of music he'd created. A few of the songs were recordings from the disbanded Gang of Five. It was one of many parties Jimmy and Luca liked to throw on short notice. There were kegs of beer and a makeshift bar with wine and hard liquor near the flotsam of furnishings at the center of the room. Cassy was standing there, along with Luca, Jimmy, and Parker.

Luca flicked cigarette ash into an empty paint can on a table.

"You smoke too much," said Cassy, sipping her wine. "But, hey, who am I to judge. Thanks for the party."

"Happy to provide. I knew you'd be a flight risk."

"Fuck off. It's not like I'm leaving the Gang of Five. I'll still pay my share of the rent and be painting here. I'm moving in with Aaron, that's all. I'm leaving my curtains and bed, the shell of my room, in case I feel like crashing here one night."

"So," said Jimmy, "our little bitch is now a *rich* bitch."

"It's not my money. It belongs to my brother. I'd give it all away just to have Victor back the way he was before the accident. Victor was my protector growing up. Now I need to protect him."

"That's noble," said Jimmy. "I was joking before. Not the bitch part. You're not about to cry, are you?"

"No." Cassy rubbed her eye and downed her wine.

Jimmy poured her more wine from the bottle he was holding, topping off his own glass. "So what's the grand plan?"

"We found a fixer-upper in Mill Valley to buy."

"We, meaning, Aaron?"

"Don't be daft. Yes, I'm moving into his little hole-in-the-hill place in Corte Madera. Once the renovation is complete or, at least, livable, we move in and bring Victor with us. We hire live-in care and whatever he needs. That's the plan."

"Impressive," said Parker.

"You'll love it. We'll be having lots of wild parties."

"Where's your other half?"

"Working late, finishing up another set."

"A set of what? Dishes?"

"A stage set, wiseass." Cassy playfully flicked wine from her cup with her finger at Jimmy, who laughed.

Luca held out his glass for Jimmy to refill it. "I will miss seeing flashes of your naked body running around here."

"Is that all you'll miss?"

"No," said Luca. "I'm sad we missed our chance to fuck."

Cassy laughed. "Like *that* was ever going to happen."

"Your loss."

"I'm sure you pride yourself on having the biggest dick, Luca, but my guess is it's as flaccid as a wet pussy."

Luca threw his wine in her face and stormed off.

"What the fuck!? It was a joke!"

Jimmy said, "You never joke about a man's cock."

"Why? Is it true?"

"Hard to say. Since I'm not gay, how should I know?"

"I thought you were bisexual."

"You little bitch. Why would you think that?"

Cassy lifted her t-shirt, exposing her breasts for a moment, to wipe her face dry. "I didn't mean anything by it. I don't care either way, you know? I'm getting a little drunk. I have no thought control when I drink. Are we still friends?"

"The night is young. So far, yes."

※

Cassy noticed her ex-boyfriend enter the room. She walked over to Oscar, who was changing the music.

"Why the hell did you invite Eric?"

Oscar looked over his shoulder. "I didn't. Look out. He's seen you. Here he comes."

"Hello, Sunshine," said Eric. He was dressed in torn jeans and a button-up denim black sleeveless shirt, looking the part of a rock star, his bare arms showcasing his numerous tattoos.

"What the hell do you want?"

"What kind of greeting is that? I want to take you back."

"I'm already taken. Thanks all the same."

Eric grabbed her arm to stop her from leaving. She pulled away from his hold. "Not so fast. We need to talk."

"No, we don't, Eric." Cassy rubbed her arm, massaging the skin where he'd grabbed her. "You hit me. Remember?"

"That's old news. It was a turbulent time for me. I don't know what I was thinking."

"You told me I was a whore. Except you were the whore."

Eric gritted his teeth, squinting as he smiled. "I'll forgive you for that remark."

"I don't need forgiveness from you. What is it you really want? Did someone tell you something about me?"

"Like what?"

"That I came into some money."

"No shit?"

Cassy huffed. "See, I knew you knew. Go away."

"You guys stole my name."

Cassy turned back. "What the fuck? Speak English."

"Calling yourselves the Gang of Five. That was *my* band. I came up with that name and I own it. You stole it! You owe me!"

"Mate," said Oscar, standing. "Hold off. I remember how it went down. All we had, including the money, went up your nose."

"Are you still a coke-head, Eric?"

He sniffed sardonically, rubbing his nose unconsciously, out of habit. "Coke had nothing to do with anything. And, no, I'm past all that shit. I've moved on."

"To smack," said Cassy. "That's what I heard."

"Listen up," said Eric. "I've got friends you don't want to know about. I need the money. If you don't pay me, they'll collect it from you, one way or the other."

Jimmy, Luca, and Parker came over to see what the fuss was all about. Luca put his hand on Eric's chest and pushed him away from Cassy, whom he was leaning into.

Jimmy said, "What's going on here?"

"This is Eric," said Cassy.

"Ah," said Luca, "the shithead guitar junkie you mentioned."

Oscar said, "He threatened us. Cassy, mainly."

Parker asked, "What is it you want?"

"Money."

Jimmy laughed. "Money for what?"

"The name you stole. Gang of Five. You're using it to advertise your art studio. It's business. I want compensation."

"I want you to leave," said Luca. "And, by the way, we're not rich artists. Far from it."

"Cassy is," Eric grinned. "Worth a million now? Gang of Five. All for one and one for all. I'll be sending you a bill. It'd be wise to make your payment promptly."

"Get out!" Luca shoved him toward the staircase.

Eric raised both hands, flipping them off. "You'll reget having done that. I got friends in low places. So watch out."

As he walked away, he turned to shout above the noise of the party, "Happy new-fucking year and post-bicentennial everyone!"

Aaron found Cassy and the other four artists standing near the bar. The vibe he was getting from the group was less than festive. He leaned in, kissing Cassy. She returned his kiss but appeared to be mentally elsewhere. "Sorry, it took longer than I thought. Are you mad at me for being late?"

"No," she said.

Luca offered Aaron a cigarette.

"Thanks, no. What's going on?"

"Her ex-boyfriend, or whatever the fuck he is, showed up here uninvited and threatened us. Targeting Cassy."

"Threatened, how?"

"You're wearing the leather jacket I bought you," said Cassy, taking another gulp of wine. "It suits you. Very boho—"

"Cassy," said Aaron. "How did he threaten you?"

"Oh," she waved her hand, spilling wine. "He wants my money. Somehow he heard about the insurance payout I received. I mean, it's Victor's money, not mine. Anyway. Shit. I need to sit down. I'm a little drunk."

Cassy collapsed on a sofa, managing not to spill more wine.

Aaron looked at the others. "This makes no sense. This guy – what's his name?"

"Eric," said Oscar. "Guitar player in the Gang of Five band."

"He has no right to Cassy's money. Why would—"

Jimmy said, "He says we stole the band's name. *Gang of Five*. And that he owns the rights. And since we've been using it to market our art gallery, he wants us to pay him for its use."

"Fuck that," said Aaron. "How much does he want?"

"He didn't say," said Luca. "I'm guessing a lot. He has no legal claim to that name. But he's a junkie."

"Heroin addict," said Oscar. "He owes people money."

Cassy pointed at Aaron. "I like you better when you don't shave for a few days. You look rugged. Handsome. Like an outlaw."

Aaron looked down at her, realizing she had too much to drink. He looked at the other four. "What do you propose we do?"

"We wait and see." Luca lit a cigarette. "It might all blow over. Idle threats and bluster?"

"Not with Eric," said Oscar. "He seemed dead serious."

"And desperate," added Jimmy.

"Eric was *lousy* in bed," said Cassy, swallowing the remainder of her wine. "Half the time he couldn't get it up. Just saying. Never trust a man who won't go down on you. *Never* would reciprocate. But Aaron... *wow*, you... you really know how to—"

"Okay," interjected Aaron. He reached down to take Cassy's hand. "Enough. It's getting late. Let's get you to bed."

Luca put out his cigarette. "I'll give you a hand."

Aaron and Luca lifted Cassy off the sofa.

"You *sly* devil you," slurred Cassy, "No way a menage en twat tonight. You don't get to fuck me, Luca. Tell him, Aaron."

Aaron exchanged looks with Luca, who shook his head, as they helped walk Cassy up the stairs.

"Tell Luca he can't *fuck* me."

"You can't fuck her," said Aaron.

"Tell him *why*."

"Tell me," said Luca, amused.

"Only I have access."

"*Ex-clus-si-vity!*"

"Got it." Luca chuckled. "Our twains shall never meet."

CHAPTER 10

2020

Birdie and Drake walked into her brother's room. It was bursting with video game noise. Flynn, Logan, and Cora were all glued to the monitor screen, focused on the exploding characters in Friendly Fire, each operating hands-on devices, oblivious to the arrival of others in the room. Birdie and Drake stood and watched the virtual slaughter of worm-like androids exploding while others escaped to devour the human attackers.

"Yes!" shouted Flynn, victorious. "Another round?"

"Hi," said Birdie, calling attention to herself. "This is Drake."

Flynn, Logan, and Cora regarded them both before returning their attention on the video game.

"Why do you like playing war?"

Flynn looked at Birdie. "Why do you like playing with dolls and stuffed animals?"

"I don't. Not anymore."

"Your stupid sweater says otherwise."

Her cousins laughed.

"I don't understand why it's fun pretending to kill people?"

"Why do you care?"

"Curious, that's all. Drake and I are trying to solve Grandma Cassy's murder."

Logan said, "You mean the serial killings? Cool."

"It's not," said Birdie. "What makes people want to kill?"

She managed to capture their attention now.

Her brother said, "All sorts of reasons. Like when I want to kill you for barging into my room, or hogging the bathroom."

"I'm serious," said Birdie.

"So am I," laughed Flynn.

"No, you're not. You're just acting out."

"We're trying to figure out the motivation," said Drake. "Why someone would want to kill a group of artists."

Flynn said, "Who are you, again?"

"This is Drake. He's a friend from school."

"Not the same school," said Drake. "I go to Tam High."

"Yeah," said Flynn. "I've seen you around."

"We met at a museum while we were both looking at one of Grandma's paintings."

Her brother regarded her suspiciously. "Whatever."

"You like pretending to kill people," said Birdie, "I thought you might have ideas on motive. Forget I asked."

"A serial killer doesn't need a reason," said Logan. "That's what I've heard."

Cora said, "From who? One of your fake-punk friends?"

"They get off on killing," said Logan. "For the thrill of it."

"If they're sick in the head," said Cora. "There's no explaining those murders. Unless the motive was revenge maybe."

"Revenge?" Birdie looked at Drake.

"The common thread was that group they belonged to. They called themselves the Gang of Five. Killed one after the other. About two or three months apart."

"Except for Grandma Cassy," said Birdie.

"The last victim," said Flynn. "Mom said she disappeared a few months after the other four died."

"Then discovered seven year later," said Drake, "On a beach in Oregon. In a sandy grave. Which didn't follow the pattern."

"All killed with a knife though," said Logan.

"Possibly with the same one," said Birdie. "That switchblade. The one found next to her body."

Logan stood, moving toward the door. "Why would the killer take her to Oregon? Was she murdered there or maybe moved there afterwards? I need to pee. I'll be right back."

Cora said, "Didn't she go crazy?"

"Yeah," said Flynn. "She had some kind of mental breakdown. Years before we were born. I was four when she disappeared. She was quirky and funny. I remember watching her paint. She wasn't batshit crazy. And she got better over time and functioned okay. At least, that's what Mom told me when I was a kid."

"You're still a kid," said Birdie.

"No, I'm not," said Flynn. "You are. Whatever made her crazy happened way before those serial killings."

"Wait," said Birdie. "What was it Grandpa told Mom? It was something Grandma said to Grandpa when he returned from a trip to Oregon? Remember?"

"Right," said Flynn. "Working in Ashland. At the Shakespeare Festival, I think. I remember now. It was weird. Mom said it was the only thing Grandma would say to him when he asked why she was acting so crazy. Something had happened to her one night. She kept repeating the same three words, over and over."

Birdie practically shouted at Flynn, "What were they?"

"'I saw God.'"

Ashwood opened his eyes and saw his granddaughter and her friend standing in front of him. He was surprised by her question which caused a turbulent rush of emotions. Beyond their two heads, he saw the painting above the fireplace – the ethereal winged angel rising as if out of the ashes of the world.

"Grandpa," said Birdie, "did grandma really say that?"

Ashwood blinked.

"She said she saw God?"

Ashwood blinked again.

"What did she mean by that? Do you know?"

Ashwood blinked. Then he slowly closed his eyes.

"You do, or you don't?"

Ashwood's eyes remained open.

Birdie looked at Drake and said, "That's a clue."

"Grandpa, do you think what happened to her, what she saw, is connected to all the murders?"

Ashwood blinked.

"Do you have any idea how?"

Ashwood shut his eyes.

She frowned, then kissed his cheek. "I wish you could talk."

Birdie and Drake walked over to the dining room table where there were hors d'oeuvres. They avoided the sushi, smoked salmon buns, and vegetables, filling their plates with deviled eggs, honey meatballs, cheese balls, and crackers. Munching on the food, they listened to the adults talking about vacation plans, making movies, television episodes worth watching, fashion trends, and such.

Blaise noticed the two of them watching and listening. "How's the sleuthing business going?"

"Pretty good," said Birdie.

"What have you detected so far?"

"Uncle Blaise, do you know what Grandma Cassy meant when she said she saw God?"

"You heard about that, huh?"

"We did. Grandpa just confirmed it."

Blaise shook his head as if attempting to shake some thought or image from his mind. He drank the rest of his martini. "I'd say what she experienced, or saw, was *not* God but Hell. Excuse me. Time for a glass of wine." He walked over to the bar.

Drake said, "Your uncle knows something."

Birdie said, "What do you mean?"

"Something he doesn't want us to know."

Birdie took Drake to a room her parents called the library with bookshelves. At the center of the room was a round glass table with an art book titled, *The Paintings of Cassandra Crow*. There were several plush leather chairs for reading. Birdie approached a display case on the wall, which held a photo of the original log cabin that stood on the property. There were architectural drawings and plans of their house, along with photos showing stages of development in the construction, and current photos. At the top of the display case were raised letters that spelled: CROWSNEST.

"Grandpa once told me he designed our house for Grandma Cassy and himself, but specifically to accomodate her brother."

Drake pointed to photos of people. "Is that them?"

"Cassy, when she was maybe fifteen, and Victor. He was older. Nineteen, I think. And these were taken later. After his accident."

"Shit," said Drake. "Sorry. He looks so different."

"Sad, isn't it? I never knew him." Birdie stepped away from the wall. "But Grandpa said he got better here. He learned how to talk, a little. And he smiled, Grandpa said. Even after what had happened to him, he was happy. That's because Victor was loved."

Birdie turned away, embarrassed by her tears.

"It's okay to cry," said Drake. "I totally understand."

"Do you want to see the treehouse?"

"There's a treehouse?"

"Of course, there's a treehouse! You won't believe it."

"Is there a dungeon, too?"

Birdie playfully pushed him. "Piss off. Why? Are you afraid we lock all our guests up and they're never heard from again?"

Birdie led the way up the flight of circular stairs that spiraled around a tall oak tree. "I hope you're not afraid of heights."

Drake clung to the railing. "How far up is this?"

"Not sure. Don't worry. Grandpa was a master builder. He said he built his first tree house when he was my age."

"We're here." Birdie opened the trap door and climbed into the wooden structure. She turned back and pulled Drake into the small circular room. It had a conical roof and plenty of head space. There were four shuttered windows. Birdie went around and opened them all to show the views.

Drake walked around to peer through each opening, taking in the panoramic sites. "Wow. This is like being in a tower."

"Or *crowsnest*." Birdie smiled, flapping her arms like wings.

"Have you ever slept up here at night?"

"Lots of times. Flynn and I used to bring sleeping bags, snacks to eat, our lanterns, and stargaze. It was amazing."

"I had nothing like this growing up."

"I told you our house was different from all other houses."

"That's an understatement. Where to next?"

"Into our underground dungeon."

Drake laughed.

"I'm serious! It's a bomb shelter with secret passageways."

Drake gave her an uncertain look. "Seriously?"

Birdie laughed. "No! You looked like you were about to pee in your pants. Come on, I'll show you my room next."

CHAPTER 11

1979

From the access road, Cassy stared up at the structure of their future home under construction.

"I guess you know what you're doing."

Aaron said, "O ye of little faith, why did you doubt me?"

"You're not Jesus. Not even an architect."

"I graduated with a degree in journalism. Same thing. I had my design and final plans signed off by a licensed architect. It's all legit. We have permits and everything. Do you like the stonework?"

Cassy began walking up the flagstone steps. She held a rolled up yoga mat under her arm. "Fantastic. I love all the boulders."

"The landscaping will go in last. The contractors just finished installing the windows and doors. The masonry crew are about to start on a stone archway over the entryway."

"What about the roof?"

"Slate tiles."

"I can't wait to go inside and see the rest."

"What's the mat for?"

"Are there any clean places to sit?"

"Probably not."

"How many acres did you say we have?"

"Three and a third."

They walked up the last flight of steps to reach the front door. There were workman's tools, stacks of lumber, a stone cutting saw, and debris strewn across the porch landing.

Cassy was wearing a favorite gypsy tiered skirt, a short t-shirt, and sandals. The summer sun was sending columns of light through the forest of redwood trees. She lifted the hem of her skirt to avoid picking up dust. Aaron unlocked the door and held it open for her to pass through.

"I love it," said Cassy. "It's so spacious."

"Cathedral ceiling for the living room." Aaron pointed to other areas. "Dining room over there. Through there will be the kitchen. Over there will be Victor's room. It will be temporary until we build his cottage with everything he'll need. I'm envisioning several bridge walkways connecting multiple structures. There will be ramps and an elevator. This is, after all, Victor Crow's home."

Cassy was staring at the fireplace sculpted from stones.

"I can picture one of your large paintings over the hearth."

"I want to live here," said Cassy, beaming.

"Well, you're in luck."

"Vic is going to love it too. Show me our room."

"Follow me," said Aaron. "Staircase isn't complete yet but it's safe to walk on. I'm thinking these steps should be polished oak with an off-white carpeted runner."

"Sounds lovely," said Cassy. "When do we move in?"

"In about six months, give or take."

"Perfect. Lead the way to the master bedroom."

As they entered the sizable space, Cassy assessed it approvingly and unrolled her yoga mat and placed it on the floor.

"What are you doing?"

"Getting naked. We're going to make babies."

As Aaron's canary-yellow station wagon entered the tunnel at the top of Sausalito, Cassy looked at him and smiled. She was feeling happy. The enclosure of darkness was brief, the archway of light seen ahead expanding rapidly, and they burst into brightness with the Golden Gate Bridge and San Francisco in the distance, far below, like a miniature city in a storybook.

Cassy began thinking of infant car seats and all the other items they'd need to purchase. She wondered if she'd be good as a mother. She watched the fog moving on the ocean as they drove across the bridge, wondering what it would feel like to have a living creature growing inside her. She looked down at the clothes she was wearing – tight jeans, t-shirt, and leather jacket – realizing they would soon be impractical for her new body. She worried about losing her slim figure and never being able to get it back again. She was letting her thoughts spin out of control, fretting over nothing that she couldn't handle, so she muttered, "*Fuck it.*"

"What?" Aaron glanced at her.

"Nothing. I love you. That's all."

"I love you back."

Her thoughts went into another spin cycle, imagining the act of giving birth, the pain, the relief, and the joy, then breast feeding a newborn. She was twenty-seven and knew nothing about caring for a baby. She needed her mother. But now she was a motherless child. She was on the verge of tears when the car stopped.

"We're here," said Aaron.

Here was Union Square. He had parked in front of the Curran Theater. Cassy checked her emotions running rampant again, gave a smile and kissed Aaron. As he exited the car, she slid over into the driver's seat. "I'll be back to pick you up a five o'clock."

Aaron waved back and she drove off.

Cassy wanted to surprise her previous flatmates and drove to a bakery near the SoMa district. She was feeling lucky, having found a parking space in front of the store.

She walked through the door, a bell chiming, which seemed to echo her tingly mood. "Morning, Freddy."

"Ah, Cassy. You're a delight to see. You look happy."

"I am. Can I have five regular coffees and a half-dozen muffins? A mix of bran and blueberry. And a container to carry it all. Oh, and we're having a gallery open house in a couple of weeks. Can I post a flyer in your window later?"

"Of course. And I'll be sure to come."

"Thanks."

Cassy took a credit card from her purse to pay. She was feeling more like a grownup. She had a sizable bank account now and she was able to pay her bills. She recalled the times when she had stolen food from a market. She left a five-dollar tip in the counter jar.

Cassy stepped aside, waiting for her order. A woman walked in and approached the counter with a baby facing Cassy, tucked inside a reverse backpack kangaroo pouch.

"She's so cute," said Cassy.

"She's a he." The woman smiled. "A handful. But thanks."

A horrible screeching, as if a monkey was being tortured, arose from across the room, causing customers to turn and look. A child who looked two years old was throwing a tantrum.

Shit, thought Cassy, I'll be dealing with that too. She picked up the container of coffees, clutching the bag of muffins, and exited the building to escape the noise.

A few blocks away was their art studio. There was now a sign on the front of the building: GANG OF FIVE. She parked, opened the back of the station wagon, picked up the coffee container and the bag, set both on the hood of the car, then slid open the metal door enough so she could squeeze through.

Cassy saw Jimmy, Luca, Parker, and Oscar all gathered by the collection of furniture.

"I come bearing gifts. And breaking news!"

Her cheerful greeting was received not as she anticipated. They looked glum, all smoking cigarettes, nodding back at her.

"What's going on? Why the gloomy faces?"

"We have news too," said Jimmy.

"Okay." Cassy set down the cardboard container. "I bought

you guys coffee. Muffins too. What?"

"I was confronted by an associate of Eric's this morning."

"Oscar is using '*confronted*' as a euphemism," said Jimmy.

Cassy noticed the bruised marks on Oscar's face.

"And?"

Luca crushed out his cigarette, reaching for another. "Well, you could say he was expressing his displeasure that we've ignored their warnings, and we've avoided paying what they say we owe."

"That's insane," said Cassy. "We own them nothing!"

"Apparently," said Parker, "your ex-boyfriend owes these drug dealers a sizable sum of money from his addiction. He told them we have money that's owed to him, so they want to collect it from us, since he's a scumbag with no way of paying them back."

"Shit," said Cassy. "What do we do?"

"Pay up," said Luca. "Or take our chances."

"How much?"

"One hundred grand," said Jimmy.

Cassy screamed, "Fuck! That's extortion. Right?"

"Bingo," said Luca.

"Eric, that fucker," said Cassy. "Goddamn him!"

Parker grabbed one of the coffee cups, popped off the lid, and took a sip. "Since we don't have the money, there's nothing much we can do. Unless, you know."

"He's not getting Victor's money! No way."

The others shrugged and reached for the coffee and muffins.

"We understand," said Jimmy. "Let's hope for the best."

Cassy felt her stomach fill with acid. "Oscar, did this asshole who confronted you say anything else?"

"Yeah. That one of us will die if we don't pay them."

Luca lit a cigarette. "So, Cassy, tell us your breaking news."

"I'm pregnant."

※

Aaron left the Curran Theater and saw Cassy parked out front in the loading zone. She was seated in the driver's seat. He tapped on the window and she looked at him with tears in her eyes, unlocked the door, and slid over into the passenger seat. Aaron sat inside, shut the door, and stared at her distraught face. She looked away.

"What happened? What's wrong?"

"Oh, not much," said Cassy. "Death threats. My ex-boyfriend's drug dealers are determined to extort money from us. And, assuming we don't pay, they said they'll kill one of us."

"One of who?"

"Who do you think? One of us who's in the Gang of Five."

"Who told you this?"

"Oscar. Some thug beat him up this morning and told him to convey the message."

A horn blast got Aaron looking in the rear view mirror.

"We have to move."

Aaron pulled out into the flow of traffic.

"Thoughts?"

Aaron looked over at Cassy. "How much do they want?"

"One hundred thousand dollars."

"Are you considering paying?"

"No. But we don't know what to do."

"The police won't get involved unless there's a crime."

"Great," said Cassy, idly tapping the side window with her knuckles. "Someone has to die first. Terrific."

"Even if you paid, I doubt they'd stop. It wouldn't end."

"My thoughts too," said Cassy. "I guess we wait for someone to die. *Shit.* Why is this happening? God–why?"

Aaron saw Cassy's tear-streaked face reflected in the window. He wanted to console her but couldn't think of anything to say that would help. He recalled the morning after they'd slept together in his car at the beach when she was fifteen years old, driving her back home. She had that defeated look again. He remembered the joy she had expressed last night when she learned she was pregnant.

"It could prove to be nothing, Cassy. I mean, it's possible these guys already know Eric is lying and has no claim to money he told them you owed him. It may not resort to killing anyone. Let's hope it's a bluff. We have to stay positive—"

"I was so happy this morning, Aaron. And now this."

Aaron had built a fire in the hearth to unofficially inaugurate the fact that they were living in their new home. Cassy and Aaron were seated on the carpeted floor, staring at the flames while eating take-out Chinese food. Aside from the crackling of burning logs, the large room was filled with silence.

"I can't believe we're here," said Cassy. She pinched a piece of the almond fried duck off the paper plate with her chop sticks and brought it to her mouth. "Hum, this is so good. And all this!" She gazed around the living room. "This feels surreal."

"Next week the kitchen appliances will be installed and you'll have your kitchen. There's more to do."

"Like a poem," said Cassy. "It's never finished."

Aaron laughed. "I don't think that's an appropriate analogy. 'A poem is never finished, only abandoned.' That's the expression."

"Fuck off," said Cassy with a laugh. "You know what I meant. Our house will be never-ending. Magical. I love it. When do we bring Victor here?"

"In two, maybe three, weeks? Once the kitchen is operational and we have the live-in nurse settled in. I want the transition to be as smooth as possible for Victor."

Cassy leaned over and kissed Aaron. "You're an angel."

"You're the angel," countered Aaron.

"A *Crow* doesn't qualify as being an angel."

"Take the compliment. You're a loving sister."

Cassy set down her plate of food and picked up her wine glass. It was a blue crystal antique item from her collection of glassware. She raised it toward Aaron who responded in kind, picking up his emerald glass of a different shape.

"To us and Victor," toasted Cassy.

Aaron touched his glass to hers and they sipped their wine.

"I shouldn't be drinking alcohol, should I?"

"A small amount can't hurt."

"I can't believe I'm actually pregnant. I feel the same. But that, I'm sure, will change."

"Have you given any thought to names?"

Cassy stared into the fire. "Blaise, if it's a boy."

"Nice. And if it's a girl?"

"Hum." She looked up at the cathedral ceiling. "Sky."

"You have my consent."

"You have no say. They're *mine*. All mine!"

Aaron laughed. "I think you'll make a great mother."

"You think? Not sure. I'll give it my best try."

Aaron pulled back the fireplace screen and used the poker to reposition the logs. It caused a burst of firefly sparks.

"Maybe Iris."

"What?"

"For the girl's name. I like that one too."

"It's pretty. How many kids do you think we should have?"

Cassy touched her stomach. "Let's see how this goes. Maybe another. Two at the most. Three might be too much."

"My parents sure were excited and happy by the news."

"Happy that I'm having *your* baby. Am I now accepted?"

"They love you. If we got married they'd be ecstatic."

"I don't need a signed document, sanctioned by the rules and attitudes of society, contrived as a God-ordained covenant and legal requirement to prove we're in love and committed. Do you?"

"No." He smiled, kissing her. "I'm definitely committed."

"Me too."

"Once we get Victor settled in, I'll start working on building his cottage. It'll have all the needed amenities and an adjoining unit for a live-in caregiver. Then I'll work on constructing an art studio for you on our property so you won't have to go back and forth into the city. Less of a hassle with a baby, or *babies*."

Cassy went silent, staring into the fire.

"You want that, right? You want to keep painting, yes?"

"Of course I do. I have no choice. Because—"

"You're amazing," said Aaron.

"Don't call me amazing. I'm not amazing."

"You're amazing." Aaron grinned, toasting her.

"Fuck off."

"Your *studio* will be amazing. Better?"

She smiled, took a bite of chow mein, then set her plate aside, shaking her head. "I'm conflicted. I don't know what to do."

"Is this about the extortion threats for money?"

Cassy nodded. "I feel responsible."

"You're not. You had nothing to do with it."

"If I hadn't been with Eric, this wouldn't be happening."

"Cassy, it's not your fault."

"Eric knows, and they know, I have the money to pay."

"It's Victor's money."

"But I control it. I don't want anyone to get hurt. Or killed. I couldn't live with myself if that happened."

ASHWOOD

CHAPTER 12

2020

Birdie and Drake were seated outside on a stone bench. It overlooked a decorative pond, fed by a stream that meandered through the property. There was a slight chill in the air, but the weather was warm for December.

Drake asked, "Are there any fish in there?"

"We've tried. The racoons come at night and eat them."

"Are there lots of wild animals around here?"

"A few foxes. And coyotes. They ate our last cat. That's why we keep Noodles inside."

"Noodles? Your cat's name is Noodles?"

"Don't laugh. Our family has had three generations of Noodles. It's a perfectly good name for a cat."

"As is Birdie for a girl?"

"Piss off. What about Drake? It's the name for a male duck. I will now be calling you Duck."

Drake smiled. "Our names are ridiculous."

"The world is ridiculous." Birdie picked up a pebble and tossed it in the pond. "Are you glad you came? Enjoying yourself?"

"I was until you called me Duck. No, I am, thanks for inviting me. Your uncle weirds me out a little. His prejudgement at the door. Another constant reminder that I'm black."

"What do you mean?"

"He thought I was a kid scouting the place to rob."

"My uncle is okay. I don't think he's prejudiced."

"If you say. I like that it's private sitting here. Not out in public where people stare and judge you. Like last week."

Birdie leaned down to gather more pebbles. "When was this?"

"You didn't notice? You probably wouldn't."

"What didn't I notice?" She aimed for the center of the pond – bouncing a pebble off the head of an angel. "Tell me."

"It's no big deal. When we were on that bench. A black kid, my age, sitting at a bus stop with a pre-teen white girl. It calls attention to some people. I was waiting for someone to call the police on their iPhone or start recording us."

"I think you might be overreacting."

"That's because you think different than most."

"People say I remind them of my grandma. Did you know I was named after her? Her pet name as a child was Birdie."

"That's cool. Makes sense, somehow."

She tossed another pebble which pinged a metal frog. "I'm glad I found your website."

"Me too."

"I like that we've become friends."

"Same here. Shall we review what we have so far in the way of clues about the murders?"

"For one," said Birdie, "the artists were killed in San Francisco, one after the other, several months apart."

"Except for your Grandma."

"Who was murdered in Oregon. Or was she murdered here but moved there later and buried at that beach?"

"All were killed with a knife."

"Maybe the same one. That switchblade?"

"Yeah. The one found beside her body."

Birdie picked up a rock. She threw it into the pond, splashing the water. "Her skeletal remains were too decomposed to reveal any DNA evidence worth anything."

"Seven years," said Drake. "Not surprising. But now we have your discovery on her paintings. Those lines by her signature."

"Uncle Blaise called them tally marks."

"She numbered them in order of each murdered victim."

"Including herself," said Birdie. "It's like she knew she'd be killed next. The last one. Number five."

"She's telling us something with each image. Each painting has a hidden message. They're all full of clues."

"I agree," said Birdie, "but to what?"

"It has to do with what she said to your grandfather."

"Saying, 'I saw God.'" Birdie tossed the last pebble and brushed her hands. "Three words. It's like a code."

"How do you figure?"

"Those words mean something specific. Grandpa confirmed it when he blinked. But then he shut his eyes. Which means, I think, he knows what she meant when she said those words to him, but he doesn't know what caused her to say it. Or what she saw."

Drake said, "I think your uncle might know."

"Why?"

"It's a gut feeling. Maybe nothing."

"No, I think it's something."

Iris fidgeted with the fabric of her dress, holding a glass of wine in one hand while the finger and thumb of her other hand rubbed the smooth silk. It was an old habit to calm herself when she became nervous or was trying to fall asleep at night. She used to rub a piece of cloth and suck her thumb. She became conscious of this childish habit resurfacing and felt a flush of embarrassment, letting go of her dress. She drank wine instead of sticking a thumb in her mouth.

Bill touched her arm. "Are you all right?"

"What? Yes," said Iris with a quick smile. "It's Christmas."

Sky was telling them all about the pilot she'd been cast in. The proposed television series was a spinoff, created after another show that had a huge run of seven seasons.

"Well," said Blaise, "maybe this one will stick and get picked up and finally make you the star you've always wished you'd be."

Sky glowered at her brother with a forced smile.

Jess interjected, "Sky is already a star. The moment I laid eyes on her, I knew she was. She's my star, anyway. Whether this pilot takes flight or not."

"Well," toasted Blaise with his glass, "here's hoping it doesn't crash and burn like all the other ones."

"Don't be an *ass*," hissed Nora.

"I'm not," Blaise laughed. "I'm teasing. I wish only the best for my little sister."

"I'm no longer *little*. But you still behave like a big bully."

Bill attempted to steer the conversation away from a quarrel and toward a congenial direction by asking Blaise, "How goes the house flipping business these days?"

"Flipped another last week. Made an easy half million off that sale. We're working already on another purchase."

Sky said, "It was generous of Father to teach you the ropes and lend you start-up money since you were broke and lacked ambition except to chase women. It launched your career to buy foreclosures and make a fortune from other people's misfortune."

"Wow," laughed Blaise. "Touché."

"It *was* extremely generous," added Iris. "You owe Dad a huge debt of gratitude."

"I have thanked Dad," said Blaise. "Jesus, why the hostility? Are you jealous that I've been successful?"

"No," said Iris. "But you should visit Dad more often. It's like you're avoiding him. You too, Sky."

"Me?" Sky looked toward Jess. "We live in Los Angeles!"

"There are things called planes. And you're not poor."

"We work our asses off," said Sky.

"You're very slim and trim," said Iris. "You've kept your figure and you're still pretty, as always. Whereas I've let myself go somewhat. I suppose I should try working my ass off more often."

Bill laughed, implying Iris made a light-hearted joke. "You both look lovely. Twin beauties. We're so happy you all made it here this Christmas. And I'm sure Aaron is pleased too."

"We have presents," said Sky. "Tucked inside our luggage."

"Therefore," joked Jess, "they're small but expensive."

Sky added, "I know you'll like our gifts."

"Ours are already beneath the tree." Blaise stretched his arms wide. "Big but cheap. I jest. Shall we open them now, Sis?"

Iris looked at her husband. "Maybe after dinner?"

"Sounds good," said Bill. "Since the kids are scattered about. Once everyone is gathered in one place, we'll do it then."

Ashwood gazed at the aberration of a diaphanous figure drifting across the living room, pausing a moment before disappearing into the painting over the fireplace. He shut his eyes to clear his mind, not sure if what he saw was real or a figment of his imagination. Cassy had spent weeks on that last painting. He recalled entering her studio to watch her. She was oblivious to his presence, brushing paint in a fury, enthralled, desperate to finish the vision she sought to capture. It was as if she'd known she had little time left. Was the translucent image Cassy? Her ghost? Were specters possible? Had she appeared to inform him of something? Or was he losing his mind?

His eyes shifted toward his children. They were adults now but he pictured them as overgrown kids. Blaise never outgrew his brazen temperament, an overly active boy full of mischief, feeling superior, being the first born. Sky was still the butterfly aware of her fluttering beauty. Iris remained the warm and fuzzy caterpillar whom children of all ages were drawn to because she had a soft touch. Cassy had been shocked to discover she'd be having twins, then loving the idea of two girls. When they were teenagers, Cassy cut from a magazine a quote by the comedian George Carlin and, with no explanation for posting the joke, adhered it with magnets on their refrigerator:

*The caterpillar does all the work
but the butterfly gets all the publicity.*

None of their children ever questioned the message or asked why she had put it there. No explanation seemed needed.

Blaise, mused Ashwood, was the boy who caught butterflies, proudly displaying them. He had a collection of their pretty wings pinned to a corkboard in his bedroom. Ashwood's eyes drifted to his daughter-in-law, Nora, whom Cassy had nicknamed Atala, after the black-winged butterfly with iridescent blue spots. Nora had been a supermodel, one of many Blaise chased after, but he'd caught Nora, pinning her down to marry him. Ashwood liked the fact that Nora challenged his son. She was a strong woman who tempered his ego. Plus, she brought an air of mystery like a dark novel.

Suddenly, his granddaughter blocked his view of his grown kids. He wanted to laugh, but couldn't. Birdie's exuberance reminded him of Cassy, along with her feisty smile. Her friend had a guarded smile. Ashwood waited as she collected her thoughts.

"Grandpa, can we ask you another question?"

Ashwood blinked.

"Do you think Uncle Blaise knows what happened to Grandma when she, you know, changed? And said she saw God?"

Ashwood held his stare, not blinking or closing his eyes.

Birdie looked at Drake. "That means he doesn't know." She looked back at her grandfather. "But he might know, right?"

Ashwood blinked.

"Drake suspects he *does* know. It's only a hunch."

She looked at Drake who nodded.

"Another question," said Birdie. "Did Grandma Cassy ever tell you what she meant with the imagery in the last five paintings?"

Ashwood closed his eyes.

"Did she ever discuss the meaning behind her paintings? Like with her earlier ones?"

Ashwood blinked.

"We think those last five paintings tell a story. Hidden messages that have to do with the serial killings. Do you want us to stop trying to solve her murder?"

Ashwood closed his eyes.

"You'll tell me if you want us to stop?"

Ashwood blinked.

"Grandma Cassy put tally marks, numbers, after each painting she created. In order of the serial killings. The first one had a dual image, like a double exposure, of a famous artist."

"Andy Warhol," said Drake.

"The other face, we think, is of the murdered artist." Birdie paused to look at Drake. "The next painting, with the number two, shows the head of a man sinking and dissolving inside a toilet bowl. This second artist who was killed had painted toilets and was a fan of – who was it?"

"Marcel Duchamp," said Drake.

"Duchamp, who was part of the art movement called..."

"Dadaism," said Drake.

"And her third painting showed a man in silhouette which was made with squiggles of yellow and ocher paint. And this third victim was influenced by another artist." She looked at Drake.

"Jackson Pollock."

"Right. And the fourth murdered artist," said Birdie, "painted only solid colors, in textures, like – who was it, Drake?"

"Rothko."

"The painter who influenced his art. And this fourth painting she did was textured, all in black, except for a dripping of red at the center. Drake and I interpret it to mean blood."

"We do," said Drake.

"And," said Birdie, "the last painting she did was huge, the one over the fireplace. She left tally marks on that one too. Number five. The fifth victim. Herself. As if she knew she'd be killed next. Don't you think all of this is important? And means something?"

Ashwood blinked.

CHAPTER 13

1979

Cassy glanced down at her pregnant stomach at seven months. She rubbed her tummy as she drove across the Golden Gate Bridge. She planned to tease Oscar because his belly was as round, but from eating and drinking too much, not from carrying a baby. Cassy liked him as a friend and appreciated his art. He couldn't draw the human figure if his life depended upon it, but his experimental use of colors was intriguing. But now he was working on a new painting that was entirely black. Minimalism to its ultimate degree, as he explained it. With the application of textured brush strokes, smooth and ragged depths of paint, when viewed at different angles the black canvas changed. Minimally.

Luca was working on a disturbing piece that he called *Perfidy*. The frame was three-dimensional, constructed of crate wood, that was intended to be hung from the ceiling in order for all sides to be viewed. It was the portrait of a grinning man, composed of torn cloth, glued to wood slats, with applications of paint. Wearing a tuxedo and top hat, his white dress shirt had a metal tip sticking through with a drop of red. The reverse side showed a knife stuck in his back. It was brilliant, but it gave Cassy the chills.

Jimmy was working on another Warholic series of duplicated faces of rock musicians. Parker was still pissing away at dribbling paint across canvases spread out upon the floor.

Cassy was eager to get to the art studio to work on her latest painting. It was an expressionist re-interpretation of Madonna and Child. The woman was naked, sitting in a red sofa while her child, a glowing infant, was curled into a fetal position and levitating before her astonished eyes. It must be something hormonal, she thought, being the reason for envisioning this image.

Cassy mounted the stairs to the second floor of their art studio, feeling the extra weight she was carrying, yet feeling buoyant, full of energy, and ready to paint. Her fingers drummed on her protruding stomach as she searched the room for Oscar but only saw Jimmy, Luca, and Lizzy standing and talking by the island of furniture.

As she approached them, she asked, "Where's Oscar? I don't see Parker either. Is there something I should know about?"

"Oscar's in the hospital," said Luca.

"Why? What happened?"

"Cassy," said Jimmy, "Oscar was attacked this morning."

"Stabbed with a knife in the stomach," added Luca.

Cassy gasped, picturing Oscar's extended belly being pierced. She placed a protective hand over her own stomach and imagined herself bursting like a balloon – deflating and sputtering around the room. She felt light-headed and sat down.

"Oh, my God. Is he going to be all right?"

"His fat belly saved his ass," said Luca, striking a match to a cigarette. "No internal organs were harmed. He got lucky."

Jimmy shook his head, brushing off his angst in a shudder, then drank his coffee. "Parker took him to the emergency room."

"They didn't call 911?"

"No, Cassy," said Luca. "Parker was nearby getting donuts. An ambulance was not going to get there faster."

"Shouldn't we go see him in the hospital?"

"He was stitched up by a doctor and released. They should both be here soon." Luca poured himself coffee. "You want a cup? You look stunned, Cassy. Like you could use a shot of caffeine."

"Here you go," said Lizzy, handing Cassy the coffee.

"Thanks, Liz. So what do we do now?"

"Fuck if I know," said Luca.

"Call the police?"

Jimmy scoffed. "Cassy, what planet are you from again? This is the real world where people die. The cops are useless in a situation like ours."

Cassy sipped her coffee. "Fuck it. I'll get the money."

"Are you serious?"

She looked up at Luca and nodded. "We'll pay those fuckers off. But we need some kind of reassurance from them. That they'll leave us alone once they get the money."

"Cassy," said Jimmy, his face grim, "when you're dealing with criminals like these all bets are off. Do you really think they'd sign a waiver and agree to go on their merry way?"

"What other choice do we have?"

Luca asked her, "How fast can you get the money?"

The cup of coffee was held in her hands for warmth. "I can have it by tomorrow. What do I do? Make a check out to 'Drug Dealers Anonymous?' *Fuck!*"

"They'll want cash," said Jimmy.

"I first need to ask Victor for permission. It's his money."

"Shit, I thought he was like... what, brain dead, or—"

Cassy stood up. "No, Luca! Victor has a mind and it's working. It's damaged, that's all. He understands me. More than you ever can or will! I need to be alone. I'll be over in my space."

Cassy sat on the stool of Oscar's drum kit. She picked up his sticks and idly tapped on the snare. On one side of the wall was his artwork. She stared at the black painting he was creating. She then turned her head to the opposite wall where her easel stood, showing a naked mother with a glowing fetus defying gravity.

"Do you want company?"

Cassy saw Lizzy standing there, model thin and tall, barefoot, wearing a robe. "It's sad what you're going through. Sorry."

"Thanks."

"How's the pregnancy? You look about ready to pop."

Cassy laughed. "It feels like that. I haven't seen you much lately. Where have you been?"

"Luca and I had a spat. We broke up. Now we're back together again. We somehow work, as relationships go."

"What do you think of *Perfidy*, his latest piece?"

"It's intense. And disturbing."

"Luca can be such a fucking *asshole*," said Cassy.

"Oh, I know. He acts all macho. But, if you want to know a secret, he's the woman. And I, you could say, become the male."

Cassy frowned at her. "I'm confused."

"When we're together. Alone. Yes, a man, because—"

"There's Oscar!" Cassy got up from his drum set. "Oscar!"

She ran over to him holding her stomach. He reached out to her and they embraced, bumping together awkwardly.

"Ouch." Oscar touched his belly. He gave her head a kiss.

"I'm really glad you're alive."

"So am I."

"I'm getting the money we need. I'll have it tomorrow."

"Seriously?"

"Yes," said Cassy. "I don't want anyone to die."

"You're an angel," said Oscar.

"I'm a Crow. There's a difference."

Cassy was talking to her belly, rubbing her stomach.

"Don't worry, Baby Blaise. I will protect you. I won't let some shithead hurt us. Okay? And one day when you're big and grown up you can protect your mommy. Do we have a deal?"

She felt a kick inside her stomach. She laughed.

"I'll take that as a yes."

She paused on the first landing, admiring the flagstones, then looked over toward the cottage under construction a distance away. She walked up the flight of steps to the entryway landing, stopping to gaze at the stone archway overhead, took in a breath and walked through the front door. She walked across the living room and into what would eventually become a den or library but was for now a place for Victor. He was in his wheelchair involved in a session with his physical therapist who was kneeling before her brother, holding a large red ball in his hands.

Cassy touched the therapist on the shoulder. "I need a private moment with Victor, please."

The therapist, a young man, nodded and stood. "Vic's doing great today, Mrs. Crow."

"Call me Cassy, please. I just need a couple minutes."

As the man left, Cassy leaned down and kissed her brother on the cheek. Victor smiled and reached out to hold her. She leaned in for the hug, then held his hand with both of hers.

"Vic, I need to ask you a favor. I need to take money out of our savings account. It's your money. So I have to ask your permission. A hundred thousand dollars. There are people who are threatening me and my friends if we don't pay them this money. It's a horrible decision but I don't want anyone to die. Do you understand?"

Victor stared at her with love and confusion, trying to process her words, frowning. "Cas-sy."

"Yes, Victor?"

"Love y-you."

"I love you too. I wouldn't ask if it wasn't really important. Is it okay that I do this?"

Victor pulled her hands to his face to kiss. "Y-yes S-sis."

"Thank you, Vic." She kissed his cheek and left the room with a stream of tears running down her face.

She ascended the stairwell to the second floor and found Aaron with a roller in his hand, painting the baby's room blue.

Cassy went over to him before he could say a word and grabbed hold of his body.

"Whoa, watch it! You'll get paint all over you."

"I don't care," cried Cassy. "Hold me, please. Promise me you'll never leave me, Aaron. You have to promise me."

"Cassy, I would never leave you. Never. I promise."

"No matter what? Even when I'm fat and ugly and mean?"

"What are you talking about? Cassy?"

She stepped away, wiping at tears. "I want us to be married. Let's get married. Will you marry me?"

"What's gotten into you? Of course I'll marry you. You've said you didn't want the formality of—"

"I changed my mind. I can change my mind. Can't I change my mind, Aaron?"

He laughed. "It's never stopped you before."

She slapped his chest, then rested her head on his shoulder.

"I love you," said Cassy.

"Do you want to marry before the baby comes? Is that it? Does it have to do with Blaise being born out of wedlock—"

"No. I don't care about all that. I want us to tie the knot here, with family and friends. Have a big party to celebrate. And I want to drink champagne and get happily drunk. So, no, to getting married while I'm pregnant and looking like a bloated whale. Okay?"

"Okay. But you're more like dolphin than a whale."

"Fuck off."

CHAPTER 14

2020

Ashwood, upon hearing the clanging brass bell, traveled back in time to 1981. He had installed the bell for their wedding day. It was Cassy's idea. She liked the concept of sounding a bell to override the chatter, gathering everyone's attention. It would not be any ordinary wedding. Cassy made sure of that. The bride and the groom would be mingling, champagne in hand, greeting family and friends before the ceremony commenced. Cassy was twenty-nine, he was thirty-three, and their baby boy one year old.

He closed his eyes and conjured images from that day thirty-nine years ago. Cassy had talked him into wearing a white and black mottled tuxedo jacket with tails, black satin vest and tie. Cassy wore a low-cut, off-the-shoulder, long black wedding gown with feathers. Blaise had been coerced into a custom-made tuxedo with suspenders. As a defiant show of independence, he removed the jacket, tie, shoes, and pants shortly after they said their vows and toddled around the house in diapers the remainder of the day followed by the babysitter. Cassy had lost her postpartum baby fat, was slender again, looking roguishly playful, elegant, and happy.

The bell clanged again and Ashwood returned to present day. He blinked, watching as the phantom crowd of wedding guests from the past dissolved into his grown son and daughters, their spouses, his grandchildren, and Birdie's guest. Seated in his wheelchair, he watched as they smiled at him. They assembled in the dining room. He was pleased to see the table setting. It was one of Cassy's ideas that had become a tradition. No tableware matched. Each glass and plate was colorful and different, having been collected by Cassy over the years from shopping at antique and thrift shops.

"Dad," said Iris. "This is Edna. She's here to help you."

Ashwood looked up to regard the frumpy middle-aged woman. She wore a string of pearls and clutched her bulky purse in front of her with both hands like a talisman.

"Pleased to be of service, Mr. Ashman."

"It's Ashwood, Edna," corrected Iris.

"My apologies. The temp agency called me on short notice with little time to prepare for this. But here I am."

Iris asked, "You've worked with stroke victims before?"

"Oh, yes. Hospice care mainly. But I'm well versed in caring for the disabled and the dying."

"Yes, well," sputtered Iris. "All right, then. Dad will need help eating tonight. I've prepared some pureed meat and pudding. He has limited muscle control and has difficulty swallowing at times, so you must be patient and careful—"

"Dear, I can manage." Edna patted Iris' arm. Just leave it to me. We'll be fine, won't we, Mr. Ashwood?"

"His first name is Aaron."

"Aaron. What a beautiful name. Shall we get started?"

Iris added, "Dad will need his colostomy bag attended to and replaced, and later he needs to be moved from his wheelchair to his bed. Bill will assist you when the time comes."

"Bill?"

"My husband, whom you met at the door."

"A lovely man, your husband."

"He is. Dad? Why don't we move you into the kitchen area. By the alcove overlooking the garden. Would that be acceptable?"

Ashwood blinked.

"Here, let me." Edna took hold of his wheelchair and rolled him from the living room into the large kitchen with Iris directing her as to where he should go. Iris then brought over the prepared meal and set it on a table next to a chair facing her father.

"Leave him to me," said Edna.

※

Birdie was seated next to Drake at the dining room table. She was pointing out all the fun facts of the eclectic dishes and glassware, explaining her grandmother's artistic vision of having no traditional sets of plates or glasses. Every item was to be unique. Some pieces were cheap, acquired when she was broke, others expensive, bought when she became rich. The idea was to make the dining experience a fun fantastical adventure, like something out of a storybook.

An antique sapphire blue water goblet was Birdie's favorite item and she was quick – as if playing musical chairs – to take possession of the seat in front of that specific glassware. She was excited that it was Christmas, watching everyone selecting seats around the table. She looked across to the living room and saw that her grandfather was missing.

"Excuse me." She got up from her seat and wandered around until she located her grandfather. Seated in a corner of the kitchen, he was facing a strange woman holding a spoon to his mouth.

Birdie entered the kitchen to observe and listen to the woman.

"Be a good boy now. That's it. Open... *swallow*. No!"

A bib had been placed around her grandfather's neck and she was treating him like a child. Birdie could tell he didn't care for her and was refusing to eat, the liquid dinner spilling from his lips.

"Bad boy! You must eat! Let us try again, shall we? No!"

"Get away from my grandfather!"

"I beg your pardon, little girl," said Edna, turning.

"I said, go away!"

"How dare you. I'm here to help."

"But you're not. You're making it worse. He doesn't like you, can't you see? And I don't like you either. Leave!"

Iris came into the kitchen. "What going on in here?"

"This rude little girl—"

"My daughter," said Iris.

"Her behavior is atrocious, Madam. She—"

"She was treating Grandpa horribly. She's a witch!"

"I am not a witch." Edna abruptly stood.

"Birdie," said Iris, "this lady is the temporary caregiver I—"

"You need to fire her. She's mean."

Iris was bewildered by her daughter's words and conviction.

"Your daughter should be punished for what she said to me."

"Please leave," said Iris. "I'm sorry it didn't work out."

Edna picked up her purse. "I've never been so insulted in all my life. I cannot work under these conditions. Goodbye!"

Iris rubbed her temples, closing her eyes, trying to think what to do. She had a turkey roasting in the oven, pans on the stove cooking side dishes. Both her brother and sister were useless preparing food, only good for doing small tasks, and no one else to help.

"I'll feed Grandpa," said Birdie.

Iris opened her eyes. Bill came into the kitchen. He was holding a bottle of wine, looking for the corkscrew.

"What's happening?"

"I fired the temporary caregiver for Dad."

"Why, Iris?"

"She was mean," said Birdie. "Grandpa didn't like her either."

"What do we do now?"

"I'll take care of Grandpa."

Ashwood was listening and watched Birdie approach him.

"Would it be okay if I gave you dinner, Grandpa?"

Ashwood blinked.

Birdie spoon-fed her grandfather.

"That woman was really mean, wasn't she?"

Ashwood blinked.

"Are you glad I made her go away?"

Ashwood blinked.

"I'm sorry we can't talk like we used to anymore."

The kitchen phone rang. Birdie wondered if she needed to get up and answer the call. Instead, her father rushed in and picked up the receiver.

"Hello? Oh, hi. Uh, sure, just a minute. Let me get her."

Birdie was curious about her father's expression, setting down the phone and going into the dining room. Her mother returned holding a serving dish in her hand, setting it on the counter. She looked at her husband, who had followed her back into the kitchen.

"Hello? Leo, is that you? Where are you calling from?"

Iris raised her eyebrows at Bill.

"Uhm, yes. She is here. Is this a good time? I don't know."

Iris began shaking her head as if uncertain what to say next to the caller, looking for help from Bill, nonplussed himself.

"Of course, you're always welcome. It'll be a surprise, for sure. No, please. I'm glad you called. It's Christmas. Uhm, I could arrange to have a cab pick you up. Oh. If that's what you want. It's a good fifteen-minute walk from downtown. We'll see you soon then."

Iris hung up and let out a sigh, placing a hand to her breast.

"I knew this would happen," said Bill.

"He's family. I had to invite him. What was I supposed to do?"

"Your heart is too big, Iris. This could end badly."

Birdie asked, "Who's Leo?"

Ashwood knew who Leo was but couldn't say because he was paralyzed. A flood of emotions gushed from his memory banks to overtake his thought for food, but his concentration was needed to regulate the neurological swallowing reflex so he wouldn't choke to death. He recalled the moment his eighteen-year-old daughter told him she was pregnant. He was still trying to cope with the shock of Cassy's disappearance. His wife was presumed to be dead – the latest victim in the serial killings of artists. All four of her friends from the Gang of Five had been murdered, stabbed with a knife. Blaise had been attending Cal Berkeley on a football scholarship but dropped out of college, turned sullen, wore only black, and spent his nights in strip clubs getting wasted.

Sky lost her virginity on prom night with her then-boyfriend and discovered weeks later she was pregnant. Conflicted over what to do and waiting too long to tell anyone her condition, unable to hide the obvious fact, it became too late to have an abortion. She sobbed uncontrollably, believing her life was over.

The decision to give her child up for adoption happened during the summer months while missing out on the post-graduation fun her friends were having. Sky was ashamed to be seen in public and hid her pregnancy by staying inside their home. It was the first time Ashwood noticed that Iris was grateful she wasn't the popular one, sought after by boys; instead receiving high grades and honored as salutatorian for their graduation class.

If there was a silver lining, it was the sibling rebonding between the sisters. Iris was nurturing, spending the summer, fall, and winter months with her twin, keeping company, and being there to support her when she gave birth. Sky named the boy Leo, then cried for days after giving him up to strangers.

Over the years, Sky had tried to erase the boy from her memory and had partially succeeded, compartmentalizing him like a fictional character in a movie or alternative world. His name was never again mentioned until two years ago. Ashwood overhead the conversations between Iris and Bill, talking about Leo. He was now a young adult and had gone on a search to find his birth mother. And at the time, Leo had been seventeen, a rebellious teen and musician, living on the streets of San Francisco with an alcohol and drug addiction.

ASHWOOD

CHAPTER 15

1980

Cassy looked askance at Aaron's announcement.

"Say that again."

"I arranged to have an exclusive exhibit of your paintings at the Falkirk Cultural Center."

She had entered their home, returning from San Francisco with Blaise tucked in her kangaroo pouch, the baby facing his father with a drooling smile. "Why would you do that?"

"I thought you'd be pleased."

"I'm not sure I am. What's the point?"

"The point is, Cassy," said Aaron, "this would provide greater exposure of your work. Important dealers and art critics will be in attendance. I want the world to know how great you are."

"Why?"

"Isn't that what you want?"

Cassy moved into the living room with Aaron following. She removed Blaise from her pouch and held him in her arms. She wiped his mouth with a tissue. "Who else will be in the exhibit?"

"They only want to exhibit your art. The curators were wowed by the photos I showed them of your paintings."

"It has to be an exhibit showing art from the Gang of Five."

Aaron sighed, "I don't think they'll go along with that."

"Then I don't want to do it."

"Cassy, I like your friends. But their art. Come on. Does anyone want to see Luca's *Perfidy*, or Jimmy's Warhol images of rock stars? Or Parker's dribbles of paint? Or Oscar's solid black canvases?"

"I don't care. It's all or nothing." She kissed Aaron. "Thank you for caring. I love you. By the way, I think you're a genius."

Aaron laughed. "Do you want a drink? I'll make martinis."

"Yes, please," said Cassy. "You're a genius because I love what you did for Victor. His cottage is spectacular and customized with everything he'll need to feel independent."

"I like to design and build things. I'm no genius."

"Take the compliment. And take your son, I'm tired of carrying him around." She handed Blaise off to Aaron.

Cassy collapsed on a sofa, kicked off her shoes, and placed her feet on the glass-topped table while Aaron moved over to the bar holding their baby.

"Watch as I mix us drinks single-handed."

"Try painting with a squirming baby attached to your body."

"I'll talk to the curators at the Falkirk. They might concede to your demands."

"It's the Gang of Five or nothing."

These gallery receptions where her art was exposed for public viewing made Cassy uneasy, so she compensated by drinking the free wine, sometimes to excess. She preferred being alone, painting in her studio, to standing in a crowded room with strangers asking her questions and gawking at her work.

Cassy put on a smile. "What was the question?"

"What were you thinking when you painted that image?"

"I try to think of nothing. A means to avoid thought."

The art critic laughed. He worked for some publication she had never heard of and wouldn't leave, hovering too close at her side like an annoying fly she wanted to swat away.

"Yes, my dear, but a glowing fetus hovering in the air before its naked mother like that. What were you attempting to convey?"

Cassy took a gulp of wine. "I really wasn't *attempting* to convey anything, because the image speaks for itself."

"Come now," said the man, poking her arm as if to prod her to reveal a truthful statement. "Was it not inspired by your pregnancy and becoming a new mother?"

"How did you know I gave birth to a child?"

"Through the rumor mill. Madonna and Child. A cute title for the piece. Were you expecting a miracle child too, like Jesus?"

"Fuck off," said Cassy, with a hint of a smile. "I know that you're attempting to be amusing. But, you see, the viewer, such as yourself, is supposed to *think* for themselves and come to their own conclusion as to what a painting means. That's the point of art."

"To be ambiguous?" He returned a salacious grin and took a sip from his plastic cup of wine.

"I suppose so, yes."

"The Gang of Five, why that name?"

"It's a long story." Cassy swallowed the rest of her wine.

"These four men you're in bed with, artistically, joined at the hip, so to speak. They all rode here on motorcycles."

"So? What are you getting at?"

"Is your art studio named after a motocycle club?"

"No, from a rock band that disbanded."

"These bikers you've associated yourself with—"

"They're artists, not thugs."

"You're far too talented to be aligned with their so-called art. It's crap. You outshine them, Cassy. May I call you Cassy?"

"You just did."

"I could do many things for you. Open doors. We should get together sometime and have a drink."

"Isn't that what we're doing?"

"I meant in private. If you get my drift."

"I do. But I'm curious. Do you put much effort into being a brazen asshole, or does it come naturally?"

His head jerked as if slapped or swatted. He composed himself, grimaced, and said, "Go fuck yourself."

"That's what I thought. You're a natural."

She finally got the man to leave.

Cassy walked over to the refreshments table to pour herself more wine. Aaron came over to stand beside her.

"Are you enjoying yourself?"

"I'm having a blast," said Cassy. "Can we leave now?"

"You need to stay. People want to meet and greet the artist."

"Maybe I don't want to meet them."

"Try to be gracious and behave yourself. Are you sure you want more wine?"

"I'm sure." Cassy emptied half the cup in a few swallows.

"Where are your cohorts? The other four?"

"Gone already. They said the gallery and its attendees were, and I quote Jimmy, 'too milquetoast and suburban' for their taste. People weren't appreciating their art. They left for the city."

"Look." Aaron began pointing to all her paintings. "Have you noticed all the red dots?"

"Meaning?"

"They've been sold. Every one of them."

"Shit." Cassy drank the rest of her wine. "I regret putting them up for sale. I like having them around to look at. It's like I'm selling my own babies. What about the other pieces by Jimmy, Luca, Oscar, and Parker?"

"I don't think any of them were sold."

"Double shit," said Cassy. "But all mine were. I'll never hear the end of it, the taunting and list of complaints. Can I change my mind and tell the gallery my paintings are not for sale?"

"Cassy, no. They're sold. Think of it this way."

"What way?"

"It will help pay for the studio I'm going to build for you. Using your own money, not any of Victor's. Guilt free."

"Well, fine, when you put it that way. Come here." Cassy held Aaron in a tight hug, kissing him on the lips. "I never thanked you for arranging all this. To make this happen."

"You just did." He kissed her back, realizing she was drunk.

"Can we go home now?"

Cassy saw Jimmy, Luca, Oscar, Parker, and Lizzy seated within the island of furniture when she arrived at the Gang of Five studio the following morning. She was hungover and a bit wobbly, lugging around a baby strapped to her body.

"Have you read these fucking reviews?"

She looked at Luca. "No. From where?" She collapsed on a sofa holding Blaise with both arms.

"The Chronicle," said Jimmy. "And other newsprints. Fucking critics. They hated us. Well, not you. You sold out."

Oscar said, "May I pour our local star a cup of coffee?"

"Fuck off," said Cassy. "Sure, thanks. It's hard to get up off this sofa with Blaise weighing me down like a lead balloon."

"When are you planning to fly the coop?"

"Not for awhile. Aaron needs time to build the art studio. And I'm not abandoning you. Once it's built, I'll still come here to paint off and on. I'll pay my share of the rent. Having to lug around a baby back and forth to the city gets exhausting. If you were a woman and not a bunch of clueless men, you'd understand."

"I understand," said Lizzy.

"Because you're a woman. Half the time."

Lizzy laughed and winked at Cassy. The men didn't get the joke and drank their coffee, brooding. Luca stood and kicked aside a can of paint on the floor to get more coffee, then light a cigarette.

"What the fuck was *that* supposed to mean?"

"Nothing, Luca, darling," said Lizzy, getting up to appease and join him in a smoke. "A private joke between us women. Isn't that right, Cassy?"

"Did I mention we're thinking of having another baby?"

Parker said, "Jesus, one isn't enough?"

"We think two might be better," said Cassy, bumping the baby up and down on her lap, getting him to giggle. "Blaise'll have a little brother or sister to play with."

"Speaking as an only child," said Oscar. "I was perfectly happy playing with myself."

"And you still are," said Jimmy.

The others laughed.

"We will miss you, Cassy Crow," said Parker.

"No, you won't. You'll be seeing plenty of me. And, like I said, we'll be throwing lots of wild parties at our house. It'll be fun, as always. Oh, and you're all invited to our wedding."

"What?" scoffed Luca. "You're getting married?"

"Didn't I mention it?"

"Yes, many times," said Jimmy. "You said getting married was for the *bourgeoisie*."

"I'm still a bohemian."

"Prove it," challenged Parker.

"We will have an unconventional ceremony."

"How so?"

"Well, Luca. Picture this. Along with Lizzy, you four will be my bridesmaids."

"Like hell," laughed Luca.

CHAPTER 16

2020

Iris was rubbing the side of her silk dress between her thumb and finger again, nervous and conflicted, unable to decide how to break the news to Sky that her birth son was about to arrive. Leo and Sky had never met, except on the day of his birth. Leo had finagled his adoptive parents to reveal enough information for him to track down the name of his birth mother. He found she was married to a successful actor in Los Angeles, and was an actress herself. To see what she looked like, he watched trailer clips of films and television series she had appeared in, available free on YouTube, and realized how pretty she was.

After an exhaustive search, by reading tabloid information, Leo discovered his mother had a twin sister living in the San Francisco Bay Area. Her phone number was easy to find, unlike his mother's that was unlisted. From Iris, his newfound aunt, Leo managed to establish a familial bond and convinced her to provide information for contacting his birth mother. He heard the surprise in his mother's voice when he informed her who he was and why he was calling. He could sense she knew he was trouble. She wished him well but said meeting in person was not a good idea. She thanked him for calling then, rather hastily, hung up.

Meanwhile, Leo continued to call his aunt, having numerous conversations before she agreed to meet with him in San Francisco. They met at a cafe where she bought him coffee and lunch. He was eking out a living as a musician, playing guitar in small cafes and on the streets. She liked Leo but realized, after spending time with him, he had an alcohol and drug problem. She encouraged him to seek treatment and promised if he did, she would find a way for him to meet with Sky. Having entered a rehab program, he was drug-free and sober, he claimed. This was six months ago, and now he was about to meet the rest of the family.

Their doorbell rang and Iris stood. "I'll get the door."

Blaise joked, "Birdie, who else did you invite?"

"Nobody. I swear." She looked at her grandfather who had been moved to a corner of the dining room, and who had blinked when she had asked him if he knew who Leo was.

"Well," said Bill, cautious with a smile, directed at Sky, "you're all in for a surprise. Please don't be angry with Iris."

Sky frowned. "Why would I be upset with my sister? Why are you being mysterious, Bill? Is a present being delivered?"

"Yes, you could say that." Bill picked up his wine glass.

Sky noticed his hand shake slightly.

"Surprise," said Iris, a quaver in her voice.

Standing beside her was a tall young man with shoulder-length blond hair, wearing a denim jacket, red t-shirt with a green logo in the shape of a tree, blue jeans, and desert boots. An acoustic guitar hung from his shoulder. His blue eyes homed in on Sky.

"Hi Mom. And family. Merry Christmas."

Bill brought in a chair for Leo, placing him toward the end of the table next to Birdie and diagonally across from his mother, who looked frozen, still in shock.

Jess leaned in to whisper, "What's going on?"

Shy shook her head, not responding.

"So," said Iris with a smile while rubbing the fabric of her dress beneath the table, "explanations and introductions are in order. This is Leo. He's a surprise Christmas present. Bill and I have come to know Leo over the last couple of years. He called unexpectedly and, uh, well, he's part of our family. So I invited him."

Blaise suddenly understood, snapping his fingers. "Aha, I got it! You're that Leo. The child she gave away."

Jess looked at his wife. "Sky?"

Blaise addressed his sister. "Wait. Jess doesn't know about—"

"No," said Jess. "I know nothing. Does someone what to fill me in? You have my full attention. Sky? Anyone?"

Blaise lifted the table wine. "Leo, can I fill your glass?"

"Thank you, no. I don't drink. I've been sober for six months. It's true, Mom. Everyone. Hi, again."

"Well, I want more." Blaise filled his glass. "Sky or Iris, I think this is your cue to talk. Unless you want me to tell the story."

"No," said Sky, looking stoic. "I will. I became pregnant in high school when I was eighteen. It was unexpected. A mistake. I was too young to raise a child, so I chose to give the baby away. I'm sorry, Leo. But I would have been a bad mother. I *am* a terrible mother."

She was unable to hold back her tears.

"Excuse me." She pushed back her chair and left the room.

Iris called out, "Sky, I'm sorry!" She got up from the her seat and followed after her sister.

Blaise sighed, "That didn't go so well. Leo, welcome. How old are you now?"

"Nineteen."

"I'm your uncle, Blaise. Your mom's and Iris' older brother. This is my wife, Nora. These are all your cousins. Except for Drake here. And this is Jess, your mom's husband."

"I know who you are." Leo nodded.

"And I will assume you already know Bill?"

"Wow," said Birdie. "Cool, another cousin. I'm Birdie."

"I know," said Leo. "Your mom has told me all about you. And your brother. One of you would be Flynn."

He raised his hand. "That's me."

"I'm Logan. Son of Blaise. This is my little my sister, Cora."

She waved from across the table.

"And this is Drake," said Birdie. "He's my friend."

Drake and Leo shook hands.

Leo addressed them all, "I'm sorry for crashing your Christmas celebration. It wasn't my intention to upset Mom. I only wanted to meet her. And all of you."

"No worries," said Bill. "Everything will blow over, calm down, and be fine. I have faith. You're very welcome here, Son."

"Thank you, Sir." Leo whispered to Birdie, discretely pointing to Ashwood seated in his wheelchair. "Who's that?"

"That's Grandpa."

"What's his story?"

"He was paralyzed after having a major stroke."

"Bummer."

Sky sat crying on the corner of her bed. She looked at Iris, who had followed her into the room.

"You blindsided me! How could you?"

Iris hesitated to sit, then did, next to her sister. "It wasn't my intention to hurt you. Leo called out of the blue and surprised me. I didn't know what else to tell him. He only wanted to meet you."

"God, I feel eighteen again. Ashamed to be alive. I'm a horrible person, aren't I?"

"No, you're not." Iris hugged Sky.

"When he called me in LA, I could tell by his voice he was drunk and disturbed. I knew he'd be trouble. So I hung up."

"That was two years ago, Sis. But you were right. Leo was an addict then, not in a good mental state." Iris rubbed her sister's back and felt they were teenagers again, and she there to console her sister when her high-flying dreams fell apart.

"Sky, he's a sweet boy. He wasn't then, but he is now. I talked him into entering rehab, to deal with his anger issues."

"Because of me."

"Not entirely. He had other issues. But his incentive to get clean and sober was to meet you. I made him a promise, that if he truly committed himself to getting better and stuck with the program, I would make sure you two met. I had no idea it would be today. He sort of blindsided me too."

Iris got up and went to the bathroom and returned with a box of tissues, handing it to Sky.

Wiping her eyes, Sky said, "Jess wanted to have children. I told him I didn't. He doesn't – *didn't* – know about Leo. This might ruin us, Iris. I lied to him. He may never forgive me."

"It wasn't a lie," said Iris, sitting beside her again. "You simply felt it best if he didn't know."

"Right. That I was a teenage mother who gave away her child because I was a selfish narcissistic *bitch*. Focused solely on my career goals to become famous. I'm self-centered. A fool. You know I am. You know me better than anyone else. I feel so ashamed."

Sky blew her nose.

"Leo is quite talented," said Iris. "I'm sure he inherited it from you. And you must have noticed how handsome he is. You passed along your remarkable genes to him."

"Talented, how?"

"Didn't you see his guitar? He writes songs and sings. Bill and I went to a cafe and heard him one night. He's good."

"A musician, huh."

"Come on, Sis." Iris stood and held out her hand. "Let's get you freshened up and back into confident Sky mode. Yes?"

Ashwood watched Sky and Iris return to the dining room. To his surprise, the first thing Sky did was approach Leo. She leaned down and wrapped her arms around him in a loving hug.

The room appeared to brighten. Everyone at the table cheered. There was laughter. Toasts were made. Their ship had survived the storm, the bad weather gone, and onto smooth sailing.

Ashwood breathed a sigh of relief. He relaxed and let his mind drift back in time. So many years, so many happy gatherings around this very table, and memories shared with Cassy.

Her thirty-ninth birthday came to mind, and he began reliving the moment, experiencing every detail.

Cassy had made a large chocolate cake with extra cream filling. It was at the center of the table. She had blown out the candles and cut generous slices for everyone, all five of them. They were wearing party hats, which Cassy insisted they put on. She was in top form, a happy mother and wife.

Their son asked, "Mom, what was your birthday wish? That you were young again and not so old?"

"I am not old," she countered with a laugh. "I'm younger than you, smart ass. Blaise, what are you now? Three going on sixty?"

"I'm *eleven*, Mom. And you're ancient."

"Ancient? How dare you. Would an old person do this?"

Cassy cupped a handful of cake from her plate and tossed it into her son's face.

There was a moment of stunned silence, then laughter. A food fight followed. It made a mess. No one cared.

A year later everything had changed. Cassy was no longer who she had been. She sat at the dining room table, expressionless, as if she'd become a zombie. Blaise had become a boy who rarely smiled, his demeanor like a clenched fist of anger. Their twin daughters were prone to cry at the spur of the moment. The home atmosphere went from a bountiful Spring to frigid Winter. And Ashwood didn't know what to do to make things right again.

Cassy told him she saw God. And that was all she said.

It took him awhile before he recalled their conversation, what she had said to him when they were young and had first met. Lying inside his station wagon, stoned, and speculating on the meaning of life and wondering if there was a God. He could not recall her exact words, but she had predicted the human mind would be blown apart if it knew the truth. If a person saw God, they would go insane.

Ashwood shut his eyes and said to himself. *Cassy, my amazing, wonderful, beautiful, crazy Cassy. Where did you go?*

A tear trickled down his cheek.

Tell me what happened to you. What did you see?

PART 3

ASHWOOD

Remember when you were young, you shone like the sun
Shine on you crazy diamond
Now there's a look in your eyes, like black holes in the sky
Shine on you crazy diamond
You were caught on the crossfire of childhood and stardom,
blown on the steel breeze
Come on you target for faraway laughter
Come on you stranger, you legend, you martyr, and shine!
— Pink Floyd

ASHWOOD

CHAPTER 17

1981

It was their wedding day. Family and friends were inside, as well as outside on the decks and strolling through the garden with glasses of champagne in hand. A bartender was serving drinks on the deck off the living room. The sliding glass doors were wide open, allowing a summer breeze to meander through. Aaron was wearing a black and white mottled tuxedo with tails and Cassy was dressed in a low-cut black feathered gown that brushed the floor. On her head was a beret fashioned with crow plumage.

Midway through the day, Cassy rang the brass gong that Aaron had installed in the living room. It alerted the guests to gather inside where Cassy and Aaron were to become newlyweds. They had asked Gina, his ex-girlfriend, to officiate and marry them. She had become a close friend to both of them, was recently married herself, and was registered as an ordained minister with the Universal Life Church. Acting as the best man was their squirming one-year-old son, Blaise, dressed in a miniature tux. The groomsmen were a group of Aaron's friends he'd known from as far back as elementary school. Cassy's so-called bridesmaids consisted of Lizzy and the other Gang of Five artists. Victor, in his wheelchair, was the symbolic father figure who gave away the bride.

Cassy leaned down and kissed her brother. Then she and Aaron exchanged a kiss before nodding to Gina to proceed with whatever she was going to say. Their wedding vows came next.

Aaron grinned. "Cassy, you hooked me on the day we met and I fell madly in love with you. I promise to be with you forever."

Cassy giggled. "I love you back, Aaron. Forever."

Gina pronounced them man and wife. They kissed again.

※

True to her word, Cassy and Aaron threw wild lavish parties at their house over the next year for the Gang of Five and many guests. Cassy liked the idea of having themes. There were costume parties, pajama parties, karaoke parties, gender swap parties, and murder mystery parties. For a neon party, Aaron had installed black lighting throughout the house. Everyone came dressed with flourescent body paints on their skin and clothing. Cassy went all out and was naked except for a thong bottom and flourescent body paint drawn to be a bikini, along with glowing necklaces, rings, bracelets, and anklets. Her face was adorned with hearts, stars, and moons.

Luca kept ogling her body, amazed at her free-spirited display of nudity, unabashed as she mingled with everyone.

"Nice body," said Luca. "You don't mind?"

Aaron shook his head with a smile. "Would it matter? She's just being Cassy. Nothing you haven't seen before."

Luca laughed. "Well, that's true. Cassy used to dash around the art studio from bedroom to bath in the nude."

Jimmy had come over to stand with them. His lips were painted green, glowing in the dark. "She's always been wild."

"Oh, look," said Luca, pointing.

Two-year-old Blaise ran across the living room holding a glow stick, chased after by the babysitter. The teenager wore body tights streaked with flourescent paint. Blaise was base-ass naked.

Luca joked, "Your son takes after your wife."

"He does like to shed his clothes and get naked," said Aaron. "It's a phase I hope he grows out before he enters high school."

Luca and Jimmy laughed, toasting to that.

It was the last wild party they had for a while. Three days later, Cassy peed on a pregnancy stick and it turned blue.

※

"Look on the bright side," said Aaron.

"What side is that?" Cassy was still in shock by the news.

"No dilemma now in having to choose which of the two names you like best for a baby girl."

"Fuck off." Cassy brightened with a smile. "Sky and Iris. I can't believe we're having twins! Not sure my body can take it."

"You'll be fine."

"Says the man who doesn't have to carry two babies inside him then deliver them through his penis."

Aaron and Cassy had arrived home after visiting the doctor for the ultrasound examination. Cassy threw down her purse on a chair and began to pace in circles.

"How the hell am I supposed to get any painting done strapped to two babies and a three-year-old son running rampant?"

Aaron came over to place his hands on her shoulders to stop her from moving. "Hey. Calm down. I have a solution."

Cassy collapsed on the sofa. "Remember, Aaron, you're not a real sorcerer. It's only a costume. And magic is fake. Okay, what?"

"Listen, with the sale of the last house I designed and sold. Plus my income from building stage sets. And your paintings also selling. Then there's our savings account—"

"Most of it is Victor's money."

"Yes, but we're in a position to employ a nanny. It would be like having a private day-care center in your art studio."

Cassy considered the idea. "I like it. That could work. When do we need to pick up Blaise from your mom and dad?"

"They'll keep him overnight. They like grandparenting. How about we go upstairs and get naked. Try for triplets?"

Cassy laughed. "Not funny."

※

Luca struck a match, raised his eyebrows, lit a cigarette, giving the news some thought, blew out smoke. "Damn. Twins, huh? Well, hell, that should be loads of fun."

Cassy waved away the smoke. "I feel a need for wine but that ship's sailed for nine months. Sorry we're late. Babysitter issues."

The Gang of Five was having another open house party. People were mulling around the large warehouse space looking at the five sections of artwork on display. Oscar was in charge of the music and came over to join the other five, including Aaron.

Cassy looked around. "It's a pretty good turnout."

"Not bad," said Luca. "Guess what?"

"I'm out of guesses," said Cassy. "Tell me."

"*Perfidy* sold."

"Wow," said Cassy.

"Congratulations," said Aaron, sipping wine.

Jimmy laughed, joining the conversation. "To a punk band with the same name. Go figure. Never heard of them."

"Twenty-one grand," said Luca. "Not too shabby. They plan to feature it in a music video."

"*Perfidy* will become immortal," said Parker.

"You'd think a knife in the back would kill him," joked Cassy, then turned serious. "Sorry. Bad joke. Any threats or appearances of those drug dealer thugs?"

Luca, Jimmy, Oscar, and Parker regarded each other, shaking their heads. Luca stabbed out his cigarette in a paint can filled with sand. He held up his index finger.

"Ah, a potential customer looks interested in one of my pieces. I must be on my way. Wish me luck."

Cassy said, "Do you think they'll stay away? Leave us alone?"

Jimmy raised his wine. "No word is good news, right? We might be in the clear."

"Let's hope so," said Parker.

"What about Eric?" She directed the question to Oscar. "Has he given up on wanting more money? Have you seen him lately?"

"Saw him recently in a bar." Oscar snapped open a can of beer. "He didn't come over to me. If he was looking for more money, he would have. He didn't look good. I need to change the music."

Someone was waving from across the room, standing beside one of Cassy's paintings.

"I think you have an interested customer," said Aaron.

Cassy walked over to investigate. She didn't recognize the man who had a long beard, but he smiled as if he knew her.

"Cassy! It's me."

"Carl? Holy shit. Is it really you?"

"It's the beard, I know." He hugged Cassy.

"What are you up to these days?"

"Still playing bass. I moved to New York. I've been in several bands. It's a living. I don't miss the old band. Only you."

"That's sweet. I've missed you too."

"Gang of Five." Carl laughed. "That name sounds familiar."

"Eric, that asshole, threatened us for money for using the name. Said he owned the rights. He owed money to drug dealers who'd threatened to kill one of us if we didn't pay. Oscar even got stabbed. I paid them a hundred thousand dollars to leave us alone."

"Shit," said Carl. "That is bad. Horrible."

"Yeah. It has been. Do you ever cross paths with Eric?"

"How the hell could I? He's dead. OD'd years ago."

"What? When?"

"Let me think. Ah, yeah. Right after the 1976 Bicentennial."

"That's not possible." Cassy looked over toward Oscar.

"Why not?"

ASHWOOD

CHAPTER 18

2020

Birdie was telling Leo how she and Drake had teamed up to try and solve her grandmother's murder.

Leo nodded. "I read about those serial killings." He took a bite of the pecan pie they were having for dessert. "After discovering who Mom was, I dug deeper to find out more about my other family, this one, surprised I was related to Cassandra Crow."

"She's your grandmother too," said Birdie.

"When did she die?"

"2001," said Drake. "That's when she disappeared."

"Her body was found in 2008," said Birdie. "Seven years later. No one knows for sure the actual date of her death."

"Leo!" said Blaise loudly. "So, you're a musician?"

"I guess my guitar gave it away?"

"He takes it with him everywhere," said Iris. "Don't you?"

"Ah," joked Blaise, "it's your security blanket."

Nora swatted her husband's shoulder. "He's not a child."

"Leo's very talented," added Iris, looking toward Sky. "And he writes original songs. You'll be impressed. Bill and I went to hear him in San Francisco."

"Play something for us," said Blaise.

Leo said, "Uh, maybe later?"

"Yes," said Sky, "I'd love to hear you play."

"You've already gobbled yours down," Iris teased her brother, "but the rest of us are still finishing dessert. Oh, Nora, thank you so much from bringing the pies."

"Baking is my new hobby."

"No," said Iris. "You baked these? Oh, so delicious!"

"Thank you."

"She is still full of surprises." Blaise winked. "Aren't you?"

Nora swatted his shoulder, this time with affection.

Birdie said to Leo, "Would you like to join our team?"

"You mean to solve the murders?"

Drake said, "We'll show you what we have so far."

"You might detect something we've both missed. Please?"

"Sure. Thanks for the invite. Count me in."

Leo was given a tour of the hall gallery, starting from Cassandra Crow's early artwork. As they stood staring at the four paintings at the end, Birdie and Drake explained how the tally marks beside her signature corresponded to the sequential deaths, and how the images related to the Gang of Five since each artist had styles patterned after other famous painters, except for Cassy.

Birdie said, "Her art is all over the house. But these are four of the final five pieces she painted before she died. The fifth, and last, painting hangs over the fireplace.

"Hard to miss," said Leo. "It's huge. Amazing."

Drake said, "So what do you think? See anything else?"

Leo scrutinized the paintings.

"Oh," said Birdie, pointing to the top of each painting. "Look here. Drake and I noticed this too."

"There's a hint of an arch," said Drake. "On all of them."

"I see it," said Leo. "Also, all canvases are the same size."

"Sort of like tombstones," said Birdie.

They looked at each other, considering her remark.

"She was angry," said Leo.

Birdie said, "How do you mean?"

"These are not happy paintings," said Leo.

"Mom said painting was Grandma's way to release and express

her angst? I think that's the word she used."

"I understand," said Leo. "But these four are different from all her other paintings. It's connected to what you discovered already. These are extremely personal. They may appear ambiguous. But it's like she was screaming to make specific statements."

"We think so too," said Drake. "They're clues."

"Grandpa thinks they may be related to the murders."

"Wait," said Leo. "I thought he couldn't—"

"He blinked," said Birdie. "which means 'yes' when I asked him if he thought so too. Any more ideas?"

"Let's go look at her last painting," said Leo.

"I see they roped you in too," said Blaise, staring up at the large canvas and sipping his wine.

"That's a fantastic painting," said Leo.

"It is," said Blaise. "I consider it her masterpiece."

Birdie said, "That rising angel is so beautiful and sad. What do you think Grandma meant by painting that image?"

Blaise said, "Who knows? The Angel of Death, maybe?"

"It's not like the others," said Leo.

"What others?" Blaise glanced around the room.

"He means the other four she painted last," said Drake.

"Oh, those." Blaise brushed his hand through the air, staggering slightly. "Never cared for them. Brings back bad memories. Best to leave the ghosts alone. Know what I mean?"

"Are you okay, Uncle Blaise?"

He looked down at Birdie and brushed her hair. "Fine, I'm fine. Too much wine? Anyway, it's Christmas. Time to celebrate life and not dwell on the deceased."

✳

Whether resourceful bees or angry hornets, Ashwood felt his mind buzzing and stirred up with memories no longer dormant. The congregation of his surviving family members, the questions raised about Cassy's unsolved death, the serial killings, the appearance of a grandson who'd been given up for adoption and was now an adult, all converging on Christmas day – he considered to be an omen.

The fact he could no longer move the vessel of his body did not help his mental state. He closed his eyes and relived the moment he returned home after a business trip to Oregon. He was excited to tell Cassy about the stage performance and enthusiasm he'd received for an elaborate set he'd designed at the Shakespeare Festival. The entire house was dark, it was early evening, and there was no sign of Cassy. He called out, announcing he was home, but received no reply. There was enough light to navigate through the interior without flicking on a light. And, for some reason, he didn't.

Sky and Iris were away at summer camp. Blaise had been invited to join his friend's family for a vacation in a cabin at Lake Tahoe. Victor had died the previous year from degenerative nerve cells in his brain failing and causing organ failure. Looking around, he noticed signs of a possible party with wine glasses left on tables and ashtrays with cigarette butts. And disturbing items. A broken glass. Torn clothing. Cassy's switchblade on the hardwood floor.

"Cassy!"

He began to worry and ascended the stairs to the second floor, hearing nothing but dead silence. He found his wife standing in the hallway in front of a full length mirror. She was naked, a robe piled on the floor behind her. She was staring at her face.

"Cassy?" said Aaron, "What are you doing?"

She didn't turn to look at him but kept staring at herself. Tears were streaming down her face, onto her breasts. He approached her, picked up the robe, and draped it over her shoulders.

"What's wrong? Cassy, talk to me."

He wrapped his arms around her in a hug but she didn't move. He gently turned her toward him. Her pupils were dilated, her green irises reduced to planetary rings surrounding black holes in space.

"God," she said. "I saw God."

"Cassy, are you drunk? Stoned. What?"

"I saw God."

"What do you mean, you saw God?"

"Aaron, I saw *God!*"

She fell into his arms like a rag doll, crying hysterically.

"Knock, knock. Grandpa, are you awake?"

Ashwood opened his eyes to a smiling Birdie. Standing next to her, on each side, was her friend Drake and his newly-discovered grandson, Leo.

"I didn't mean to startle you. Did I?"

Ashwood closed his eyes.

"Good. We have more questions. Is that okay?"

Ashwood blinked.

"Leo has joined our team. He's been helpful. We may be getting closer to finding answers. Isn't it cool that you have a new grandson? And I have a new cousin. I'm happy, aren't you?"

Ashwood blinked.

"Aunt Sky wasn't so happy," said Birdie. "Not at first."

"I shocked Mom," said Leo. "I think she's starting to accept me. Even liking the idea that I'm here. What do you think?"

Ashwood blinked.

"That means yes," said Birdie. "Grandpa, I hope this doesn't upset you. It's a question about that knife. The one that was found next to Grandma's body."

"The switchblade," said Drake.

"Does that knife mean anything to you?"

Ashwood blinked.

"Oh, my God," gasped Birdie, excited. "It's another clue!"

Drake said to Leo, "It has to be a yes or no question."

"That switchblade," said Leo, "you'd seen it before?"

Ashwood blinked.

"Holy shit," said Birdie. "Sorry. Wait. Was it Cassy's? I mean, Grandma's knife?"

Ashwood blinked. Then closed his eyes.

"It was or it wasn't? I'm confused," said Birdie.

"Okay, let me think," said Leo. "It was someone else's knife? But she took it? Or, maybe, it was given to her?"

Ashwood blinked.

Birdie looked at the others. "Let's ask Uncle Blaise."

As the three of them left, Ashwood closed his eyes, troubled by the memory of seeing the switchblade lying on the living room floor, and finding Cassy crying in front of the mirror.

The knife blade had been flipped open.

CHAPTER 19

1982

Upon hearing that Eric, her ex-lover, had died from an overdose in 1977, shortly after he'd threatened her, she became plagued with a burning suspicion of betrayal. She asked Carl, former bass player for the Gang of Five band, not to tell Oscar that she'd been told Eric was dead. Carl was puzzled by her request, agreeing to say nothing to Oscar, but wanted to know why. She told him it was a matter of life and death, so he kept his word.

Cassy didn't want to believe what she now suspected. She didn't want to believe she'd been lied to and deceived. If true, who else among them knew Oscar screwed her out of one hundred thousand dollars? Were they all complicit? Were the threats from drug dealers even real? She was conflicted. It caused a fissure in the tight bond of friendship between her and the Gang of Five artists.

Luca was helping Cassy carry a stack of canvases out of their art studio and placing them into the back of her station wagon.

"You haven't been around lately," said Luca.

Cassy indicated her pregnancy. "Motherhood has put a crimp in my former lifestyle. It's a leave of absence. I'll still be paying rent."

"We've missed you, that's all. Don't be a stranger."

They hugged. As Luca stepped back, he placed his hands on her stomach, rubbing her enormous bulge of flesh and shaking his head. She felt a twinge of deep sadness as he kissed her cheek.

"Thanks for your help, Luca."

"Good luck with these two. Keep us posted. My offer to be their Godfather still stands."

Cassy laughed. "Sure, I will let you know. Bye."

Cassy had driven only a few blocks away before realizing she'd forgotten to take her set of canvas pliers. She returned to the studio warehouse and parked by the door. She paused to catch her breath, feeling the pressure of carrying two babies inside her, exhausted, and eased out of the car. Inside the entryway, she stopped upon hearing voices from above. They were by the stairwell, gathered there, doing something. Luca, Jimmy, Oscar, and Parker were talking about her. She froze when she heard her name spoken.

Jimmy: "Cassy is no longer one of us. Face it, she's gone."
Parker: "She flew the coop like you said she would."
Luca: "That exhibit she orchestrated in Marin was a joke."
Oscar: "It was a fucking disaster."
Parker: "I think she arranged it to make us look bad."
Oscar: "She wouldn't do that, Parker."
Parker: "Oh, really? Remember the fucking reviews!"
Jimmy: "Those suburbanites loved her art. They hated us."
Luca: "We're too edgy for their vacuous tastes."
Parker: "Our little bitch sold out. Literally and figuratively."
Jimmy: "What did you expect? She's a conniving chick."
Oscar: "Come on, guys. Cassy's talented. And—"
Luca: "Full of herself. She believes she's superior to us."
Oscar: "Give her some slack, Luca."
Luca laughed: "Slack? Like you did? Don't be a wuss."
Jimmy: "We all benefited. Are you having regrets, Oscar?"
Oscar: "Cassy's money saved our broke asses. Admit it."
Luca: "A hundred grand taken from a million is nothing!"
Parker: "Get over it, man. What's done is done."
Jimmy: "Oscar, she's still a rich bitch. And none the wiser."

Cassy left the building with tears streaming down her face. She squeezed into her car and felt sick, her swollen body about to burst. She drove off screaming, *"Fuck! Fuck! Fuck them all!"*

Cassy nearly died giving birth to her twins during an emergency preterm cesarean delivery. Sky was in breech position with Iris lying next to her sideways. Aaron was holding Cassy's hand and trying to comfort her when the alarms came on, alerting staff to a clinical change of plans, requiring immediate action.

Aaron was pushed aside, alarmed too by the rush of nurses who entered the room, there to assist as the doctor sliced open his wife's abdomen with a scapel. He watched as one baby, followed by the next, was extracted. Cassy's enlarged placenta and over-distended uterus caused excessive bleeding to occur. Aaron was told to leave the room as they frantically worked to stop the hemorrhaging and save Cassy's life.

Aaron was taken to a room where his parents had been waiting. They held their distraught son who feared he might lose Cassy, a fate he couldn't imagine or endure. Time seemed to dissolve. Eventually, he was informed her vital signs had stabilized, but she'd lost a critical amount of blood and was in the ICU. After visiting Cassy, he visited their newborns who were in the neonatal intensive care unit.

The shock and anxiety settled into a thankful relief as Cassy gained her strength, along with their preemies, and Aaron was able to take the twins and mother home after a stressful several weeks.

Having survived the ordeal of giving birth to twins, Cassy cared little about her art, only about lying in bed and nursing her two girls. They hired a nanny to help out and watch after Blaise who was now a three-year-old ball of energy. Aaron took a break from work but, after a few weeks, was back overseeing the construction of Cassy's art studio, remodeling a house for resale, and designing stage sets for two theater companies.

Aaron entered their master bedroom late one afternoon, finding Cassy propped up in bed with each of her breasts fully occupied by a suckling baby and a smile on her face.

"Welcome home, Daddy."

"And how are things with Mommy?

Aaron sat on the bed and leaned over to kiss her.

"Mommy and babies are fine. These ravenous little buggers are sucking me dry. My nipples are sore. Besides that, things are great. How is your day going?"

"Good." He picked up a greeting card, one of several, placed on her nightstand. "I see the Gang of Five sent you well wishes."

"Hum," said Cassy. "I wish them well too."

"You haven't invited them over for a visit to see the babies?"

"No."

"Why not? What's going on?"

"Not sure."

"About?"

"Them."

"Do you care to elaborate?"

"No."

Aaron stood, puzzled. "If you want to talk about whatever it is that's bothering you, with them, you'll let me know?"

"I will."

Cassy blew Aaron a kiss, refocusing on her breastfeeding twins.

At six months, the twins were commando crawling across the living room floor, guided away from reaching their mother by Lena, their nanny, as Cassy composed herself for an interview with OMNI Magazine. Aaron had been actively promoting her art and arranged to exhibit her paintings in several San Francisco Bay Area galleries.

Cassandra Crow was rising as a recognized name in the art world as her paintings continued to sell and gain the attention of critics eager to know more about her. Cassy loved that people were appreciating her art but hated both the fawning attention and diagnostic scrutiny these images she created were receiving.

Aaron wanted to be in the room during the exchange between interviewer and artist but their three-year-old son who had learned to make farting noises, which caused him to giggle and call attention to himself, had forced Aaron to vacate the premises with Blaise. Therefore, he missed Cassy's remark that caused some consternation among her group of artistic friends.

"Your history fascinates me, Cassy. May I call you that?"

"Yes, it's my name."

"Is it true you were a teenage runaway?"

"True. I ran away from home at the age of fifteen."

"To pursue a career in art?"

Cassy laughed. "Not exactly. The motivation was to escape a toxic home environment."

"Would you care to elaborate?"

"Not really."

"Can we return to that subject later?"

"Maybe. Let's see how this goes."

The interviewer looked at her notes. "For a short period after arriving in San Francisco in 1967 you lived in the Haight Ashbury district at a communal house with a group of musicians?"

"True again."

"Creating poster art and going on tour with a rock band?"

"Yes. It wasn't the best use of my time."

"Regarding your artwork?"

"That too."

"After traveling with this band, you then formed an art studio in SoMa with four other artists. All men who were much older than yourself, still a teenager, at seventeen?"

"What's your point?"

"Your relationship with these other—"

"Friends. A platonic relationship. We didn't *fuck*, if that's what you were getting at."

"I wasn't angling to—"

"Yes, you were. It's okay. Go on."

"And you named yourselves, this group, the Gang of Five?"

"Correct."

"A name you took from the defunct rock band—"

"It was ours to take. Nobody had a claim to that name!"

"I wasn't implying they did."

"Sorry. What were you asking?"

"Are you still associated with the Gang of Five art studio?"

"We're sort of on an hiatus."

"Because of these new additions, your twins?"

"Sure. I guess."

"You had a conversation with James Norton, another art critic. He works for Artwalk magazine. You met at the Falkirk exhibit."

"Refresh my memory."

"He said you were somewhat rude to him."

"Sounds like me. I might have had too much to drink."

"Do you agree with his assessment of your art? He said, I quote, 'Cassandra's visions reflect the origin of her name. Like the Trojan princess gifted with prophecy, her art shines and excels over men.'"

"No comment."

"Okay." The interviewer smiled and glanced at her notes. "It's reported you almost died giving birth to your twin daughters. That must have been frightening. Is it true?"

"Yes, true. But there are worse things in life than dying."

"Really. Such as?"

"Betrayal. Were you going to ask me about my paintings?"

CHAPTER 20

2020

Birdie wheeled her grandfather back into the living room. She crouched beside him to listen to the music. The entire family had gathered on chairs and sofas to hear Leo, who had been asked to play something on his guitar.

"This is a favorite of mine," he said with a nervous smile, tuning his instrument, then strumming. "I'll play you one of my own songs, but I'll start with this by Kris Kristofferson, made famous by Janis Joplin. Hopefully, I can remember the words."

Ashwood closed his eyes. The music took him away to another place and time. Back to when he was in college, driving alone in his Peugeot station wagon on a mountain road beside a river, looking for solitude. While missing Cassy, this song played on a casette tape.

Freedom is just another word for nothin' left to lose
Nothin', and that's all that Bobby left me, yeah
But feelin' good was easy, Lord, when she sang the blues
That feelin' good was good enough for me ...

Ashwood opened his eyes, noticing Leo's change to the lyrics, from a he to a she who was singing the blues. He smiled in thought and closed his eyes, recalling how he had turned his head to look for Cassy, imagining her beside him in the passenger seat but, of course, she wasn't there. She had left, searching for freedom, venturing alone to somewhere far away. San Francisco? He knew he had to find her but wondered if he ever would. She was fading into a dream.

Ashwood opened his eyes when he heard the sound of clapping, awakening him from his reverie.

"Wow," said Birdie, looking at her grandfather. "Leo is really good. Don't you think?"

Ashwood blinked.

Leo began to play a song he had composed.

As Ashwood listened, hearing the haunting melody, he stared at the large painting on the wall. He wondered, did Cassy create this rising angel as a parting gift? As a remembrance of who she had been and where she was going next? A search for freedom, somewhere far away?

Ashwood felt Cassy's presence again, as if watching over them from the painting above the fireplace. He thought of the time she had talked about angels. Their son and daughters had been teenagers, and they were picnicking on Mt. Tamalpais. Above, high upon the mountaintop, it was a warm and sunny day. Below, the entire world was covered in a layer of fluffy white clouds and fog.

"We're angels," she proclaimed. "We've reached heaven!"

Iris asked, "Do you believe there's a heaven, Mom?"

"No." Her burst of manic enthusiasm was suddenly gone.

"When you saw God, is this what you saw?"

Cassy regarded Sky, who had asked. "Nothing like this. This is beautiful. But not real. Nothing is. And God is not to be seen."

"Except you did," said Blaise sullenly, staring at her.

"And look what it did to me."

Sky said, "But, Mom, be happy, you're famous."

"And look what it did to me."

"I suppose I'm to blame."

"Your Dad's right. I never wanted it. But he promoted me into being a star. I was happy before all *this*. Yet, I forgive you."

Ashwood recalled the kiss as she leaned over and took hold of his face, pressing her lips to his. An intense kiss lasting too long and feeling awkward in front of their kids.

It felt like a parting kiss, the kiss of death.

When Ashwood opened his eyes again, time had passed and his family was opening presents. Birdie was busy playing Santa's helper by passing around the marked gifts, selecting them one by one from under the tree. A variety of garments, gadgets, and gift cards were unwrapped and displayed. Past Christmases flashed before his eyes with a rush of emotions. The happy and sad times converged into a glittering ball of reflective memories, spinning like an atomic planet, signifying a life fully lived, all bound into the blink of an eye.

"Leo," said Sky, "I'm sorry I have nothing for you."

"Not true, Mom. You're my gift. Finally knowing you."

"That's so sweet." Sky rose from her chair. "I don't deserve you, Leo. I don't. Thank you. Come here, Baby. Give me a hug."

A lovely moment. Ashwood was glad he was able to witness this reuniting of Sky and the child she had given away. He shut his eyes again, drifting into stirred-up memories caused by Birdie's quest to find answers to Cassy's death. The fold-up camping shovel and empty bottle of vodka found beside her skeletal remains resurfaced to haunt him. Detectives had asked him about these items. Did he recognize the shovel? He did not. Did the vodka bottle bring to mind anything? She liked to drink vodka. That was all the information he could provide.

It wasn't until days later that he vaguely recalled a purchase Cassy had made several years before her disappearance. He had been reviewing the transactions on their charge card statement, and he didn't recognize a purchase from a hardware store. He asked Cassy. She told him it was a cute little shovel she liked and thought they'd want the next time the family went camping. He couldn't recall the last time they'd gone camping, but thought nothing odd about it because she sometimes bought things they never used. The first time he saw the shovel was at a family beach outing one day.

He didn't mention this recollection to the detectives because the implication of it possibly being the same shovel, found buried with her body, was too disturbing. One explanation for the shovel being there was too painful to comprehend. Especially when he was told the location where her remains were found. He knew the exact spot. How could the killer know what that beach meant to them?

"Knock, knock. Anyone home?"

Ashwood opened his eyes to his smiling granddaughter.

"Merry Christmas. This is my gift to you, Grandpa."

It took Ashwood a moment to adjust his focus on the image he was seeing held before him. A pencil drawing on paper showing two faces he recognized. Cassy and himself, when they were younger, maybe in their twenties or thirties, happily smiling.

"I drew it in my art class. It's from a photo of you and Grandma that I found in Mom's family album. I know it's not very good. But I'm getting better. I want to be an artist like Grandma. Do you think it's any good?"

Ashwood blinked.

"Grandpa, why are you crying?"

Blaise was seated on a couch, looking down at the silver tie clip held in his hand, his fingers rubbing the miniature rectangular glazed self-portrait of his mother.

"It's from one of her paintings," said Birdie. "It was my idea as a gift for you. Do you like it, Uncle Blaise?"

He looked up with watery eyes. "Very thoughtful, Birdie. Yes, thank you. What's going on?"

Standing next to her were Drake and Leo.

"We have a question to ask you."

"Another?" Blaise smiled. "Okay, fine. Shoot."

"It's about the switchblade knife found next to Grandma."

"Jesus," said Blaise, rubbing his forehead. "What is it you want to know?"

"Did you know about that knife?"

He looked up at Leo. "Know about it, how?"

Drake added, "Had you seen it before?"

"Many times," said Blaise. "Assuming it was the same one she kept in a drawer and had gone missing."

"Where was the knife kept?"

Blaise stood. "Christ Almighty, what difference does it make? It was kept in the living room." He pointed. "Over there, in that small antique table that has a sliding drawer."

Birdie asked, "Was the knife hers?"

"It was her brother's. As the story goes, the way I heard it told. She stole it first, before he gave it to her. She took it for protection when she ran away from home at age fifteen."

"That's ballsy," said Leo.

"Yeah, well," said Blaise, "that was Mom."

"When did you notice the knife was missing?"

Blaise was losing patience with all the questions, but answered Leo, placing a hand on his shoulder. "When her remains were found with that knife, okay? I never thought to open the drawer and look to see if her knife was still there. Why would I?"

"I would have been curious to know," said Drake.

"Well, I'm not you. Besides, those switchblades are available in stores and online everywhere. They're not unique."

"I'm sorry we upset you, Uncle Blaise," said Birdie.

"It's okay. Why don't you ask about the abandoned car?"

"What car?"

Blaise sat on the shoulder of the couch. "I was impressed those detectives discovered this possible evidence connected to her murder. When her body was found after seven years, investigators reopened her case and searched Oregon police records for suspicious incidents, any reports taking place by that beach the year she went missing."

"In 2001," said Drake. "And?"

Blaise attached Birdie's gift to his tie, "Bingo! There had been reports of an abandoned car, a Volkswagen Beetle, parked along the beach for weeks. The police had it towed away."

Leo said, "And?"

"Get this. I can't believe they dug this up. The car had been owned by a man who lived in Mill Valley."

"*Shit*," said Birdie. "Sorry."

"That was pretty much my reaction too. A strange coincidence? The detectives then investigated the owner. He'd been dead for three years. His widow said he'd sold the car years ago. And, sure enough, records existed showing he'd notified the DMV of the sale. He put down his daughter as the new owner. And, guess what, who do you think his daughter was? The *nanny* we had as kids."

Blaise stood. "Unfortunately, it led to another dead end."

"No," said Leo. "What about this man who had owned the car? Your nanny's father. Who was he? What did he do for a living?"

Blaise sat back down. "He had a janitorial service. And, again, coincidentally, many of his clients were art galleries and museums."

"That's a major lead," said Drake.

"That's what the detectives thought. But nothing came of it. He had alibis for his whereabouts during each murder – posthumously, from his widow and others. Plus, his daughter claimed she never saw or owned the car. She even passed a lie detector test."

"That man could have been the serial killer," said Birdie. "And what about your nanny? What happened to her?"

"Who knows?" Blaise rose off the couch again. "Anyway, let's try to focus on a merry Christmas. Stop chasing windmills."

Birdie, Drake, and Leo watched Blaise move over to the bar.

"I don't get it," said Birdie. "Windmills?"

"Don Quixote," said Drake. "From that novel. It means stop seeking something that's unobtainable."

CHAPTER 21

1986

Cassy had chosen Lena to be their nanny over other applicants for several reasons. At the time, she was nineteen, enrolled in night courses at the College of Marin, an aspiring artist who studied art history, lived nearby with her parents in Mill Valley, said she loved babysitting children since she was fifteen, was pretty, and reminded Cassy of her better self. The alternative self she imagined she could have been had she not run away from home, dropped out of school, taken drugs, lived and toured with a rock band, used foul language without forethought when expressing herself, and killed a man with a switchblade.

They were outside standing next to one another in the garden, each pushing one of the three-year-old twins in a swing. Sky and Iris were screaming with delight, wanting to go higher and higher. Cassy turned to smile at Lena, who smiled back. She made Cassy think of the character from the movie *Snow White* for Lena, too, had bluish-black bobbed hair, dark brown eyes, long eyelashes, and a smile that evoked innocence. Then again, Cassy mused to herself with wicked humor, Lena could be an axe murderer hiding within the guise of a sweet-faced, virtuous girl.

Cassy nodded to Lena and brought Sky to a hault by grabbing hold of her chair when she swung back. Lena did the same with Iris.

"Mom, *no*," whined Sky. "More!"

"More!" Iris echoed.

"You've both had enough," said Cassy.

"Your little girls are twin bundles of energy," said Lena. She unfastened Iris, removing her from her swing seat. "What should we do with them next?"

"Tie them to a tree so we can get some rest?"

Lena giggled. "Cassy, you're terrible."

"I am, aren't I?"

Sky squirmed, shrieking with laughter, as Cassy tickled her, then lifted her into her arms, setting her down on the ground.

"It's close to their lunch time," said Lena.

"Good idea. I'll find Aaron. He's out front somewhere teaching our daredevil son to ride his bike. I'll have Blaise sent to the kitchen and then set up the kids' easels. I want to get to my painting."

Lena bent down to address Sky and Iris with widened eyes in a show of excitement. "Girls, who wants to finger paint after lunch?"

Both Sky and Iris jumped up and down raising their hands.

"Then get your butts inside pronto." Cassy playfully swatted their behinds and turned to Lena. "I'll meet you in the studio."

"I'll make peanut butter and jelly sandwiches," said Lena. "And give them milk with slices of apple. Is that all right?"

"You're an angel," said Cassy.

Having taken time off from her artwork nursing two babies and nurturing infants, Cassy was back into the rhythm of painting on a regular schedule. She was becoming prolific again and able to enter the creative zone with greater ease now that she had a reliable friend in her nanny, Lena, to help her oversee and entertain the children. To hone her illustrative skills, Cassy first painted portraits. She'd painted the faces of all her children, also Aaron, Victor, and Lena. She was presently working on a self-portrait. Once completed, she planned to focus her attention on a large unfinished piece showing a naked woman with wings prepared to take flight off a seacliff.

"I recognize that woman," said Aaron, entering her studio.

"I'm attempting to make myself look better than I am." Cassy stepped away from the self-portrait, frowning at her image.

"Impossible." Aaron gave her a kiss.

"What are you up to?"

"Not sure. Taking the day off. Maybe work on the treehouse?"

"The kids will love it," said Cassy, dipping her brush into red paint on her pallete, then dabbing it into the ochre.

"Hi, Daddy," said Iris.

"Look what *we're* doing." Sky showed fingers full of color.

Aaron came over to the day-care corner of the room with the small easels and an assortment of toys. "Hi, Lena."

"Hi, Aaron."

"Time to see what our precious geniuses are creating." Aaron stared at their canvases dripping with color. Sky, he could discern, had drawn a bird flying over flowers. The swirl of colors and the blob Iris had formed with her fingers had the possible semblance of an animal.

"I give up," said Aaron. "Is that a rabbit?"

"*Daddy.*" Iris scrunched her face. "It's Noodles!"

"Oh, yes. I see our cat now. Very nice."

Iris smiled, pleased, returning to finger painting.

Aaron moved over to look what his six-year-old son was doing with his fingers and paint and saw the mess. The entire art paper was covered and soaked with blue, black, purple, brown, red, green paint dripping onto the dropcloth protecting the floor.

Aaron laughed and said to Cassy. "Beware! Your son has gone over to the dark side and become an abstract artist."

Blaise, face smeared with paint, frowned at his father.

"Nice work, Son."

"I'm done. Dad, can I watch you build the treehouse?"

"Sure. After I visit your Uncle Victor. I think he might like to come outdoors to enjoy the day and watch too."

Lena removed Blaise's smock. "I'll get him cleaned up and then send him outside to you."

"Thanks, Lena."

"Of course." Her dark brown eyes and bashful smile lingered on him before looking away, guiding Blaise over to the sink.

✷

As Aaron walked into their bedroom, Cassy came out from the bathroom and said, "I can see how you look at her."

"What are you talking about?"

"Don't play dumb," said Cassy. "Lena."

"What about her?"

"Do you want to fuck her?"

"Cassy, seriously?"

"Yes, seriously. You've never thought of fucking her?"

Aaron took off his coat and hung it in the closet. "Well, if you want me to be perfectly honest."

"Please."

"I do imagine, occasionally, what it would be like to fuck other women I happen to see. Some celebrity, for example. Or a pretty woman as she walks by me. Because I'm a man who is attracted to women. Always have been. But that's as far as it will ever go, as a fleeting fantasy, because you know why?"

"I'm listening."

"Because I love you, Cassy. You are the love of my life and I am committed to you. We made a promise to each other. Exclusivity."

She came over and put her arms around him.

"What's this all about, Cassy?"

"I'm feeling insecure, I guess. No longer sexy."

Aaron hugged her then pushed her away to look her in the eyes, brushing hair off her face. "You're sexy. Trust me."

"I feel fat. With an ugly scar across my stomach."

"You're not fat. And I've never seen a more sexy scar."

She slapped his chest and smiled. "If you ever fuck our nanny I will die. Kill you first, then myself."

Aaron laughed. "Then you have nothing to worry about."

"Promise?"

"I promise," said Aaron. "I like Lena very much but, if you've noticed, it's the way she looks at me sometimes. A little flirtatious. She may not be as innocent as she comes across."

"She's twenty one. I wouldn't expect her to be virginal."

"You know what I mean. But she's great with the kids and they love her. And so do we, as a member of the family, so let's leave it at that. Are we all good again?"

"All good." Cassy gave him a kiss.

There was a soft knock. Aaron went over and opened the door. Lena was standing there holding her coat.

"The kids are all set, eating their dinner in the kitchen. I'll be going now. I have a class in an hour."

"Thanks," said Aaron.

"Lena," said Cassy, "can I have a word with you in private?"

"Sure, what is it?" She walked into the room.

"I guess I'll be leaving." Aaron closed the door behind him.

Cassy was blunt. "Do you intend to fuck my husband?"

Lena's snow-white face turned scarlet. "Excuse me?"

"It's a simple question. He's a handsome man."

"Yes, but, no. Am I being fired?"

"You're not being fired. But I don't want you thinking you can fuck him. Because you can't. Understood?"

Lena nodded and began to cry.

Cassy came over and hugged her. "Sorry, Lena. I can be a bitch. I'm feeling vulnerable and overly protective. We really love you and consider you part of our family."

"Me too."

"And we value who you are. Believe me, we do."

"Thank you." Lena wiped at her tears.

"Do you need to leave right away?"

"No, I can stay and talk if you want. I'm not in any rush."

"Speaking of family." Cassy sat on the bed and gestured to a chair which Lena took to mean she should sit. "I feel bad I've never asked about your family. How's your mom and dad?"

"They're fine. My mom's a homebody. She likes to cook and work in her little garden. My dad's kinda weird but I love him."

"I've seen you come and go in a variety of cars. I think I've seen you driving five different makes and models."

Lena laughed. "That's my dad. His hobby is buying used cars, fixing them up, then selling them. For extra money."

"What does your father do?"

"He owns a janitorial business. Which is a joke since our own house could use his services."

"I don't even know where you live."

"You can't miss it. It's the house off the main road leaving Mill Valley. There's junk piled everywhere. Dad's been cited by the city to clean up the mess. Neighbors have complained."

"I think I know the house. I'm sorry, if it's that green one?"

"It is. I can't complain too much because, in a way, he's the one responsible for putting me in touch with you."

"Really? How is that?"

"His company does contract work for several art galleries and museums in the city. He knows who you are and likes your artwork. He's the one who noticed your ad on the bulletin board and said I should call. So I did, and now here I am! Crazy, right? Unexpected luck. It was fortuitous? There's another word for that."

"Serendipitous?" said Cassy.

CHAPTER 22

2020

Cora and Logan wandered back with Flynn upstairs to his room to play video games. A cat was curled between pillows on his bed.

"Oh, look," said Cora, "Noodles has resurfaced!" She walked over, scooping into her arms the tabby who murmured discontent before accepting his capture, followed by purring as his tiger-striped fur received strokes of affection. "You're a recluse, aren't you?"

Flynn took possession of his plush desk chair, rocking back and forth as he spoke, "Noodles is not a party animal. He hides out in here or in Birdie's room when we have guests."

Noodles snarled, fidgeting in her arms, and Cora dropped him to the floor. "He's not much of a people person either."

"He's just being a cat." Flynn leaned back, brushing his longish hair as he stared at Logan. "You're no longer the oldest cousin. Leo bumped you out of your spot."

"As if I give a shit," said Logan, sitting on the bed. "He's good on the guitar. I give him credit for that."

"What's with your hair, man? Mohawk, really?"

Cora laughed. "He's an Indian turned punk."

Logan stroked his shaved head. "My friends and I decided to say 'fuck it' and be different. My dad hates it."

"There you go," said Flynn. "Makes more sense now."

Cora said, "What about you?"

"What about me?" Flynn squinted, waiting for it.

"Your *too-cool-for-school* look. Shaggy blond hair, torn jeans, and matching hoodie. The girls must love you."

Flynn scoffed, grinning. "It feels good to be loved. Sorry I didn't get dressed up for prom like you did, Cora."

Logan laughed and high-fived his cousin.

Cora blushed. "It was Dad's idea that I wear this dress."

"He even bought the dress for her," said Logan.

"Sick," said Flynn. "That said, it looks really good on you."

"Thanks?" She smiled self-consciously.

"It's too bad you're my cousin."

"What's wrong with me being your cousin?"

"Don't you get it, Sis? So he could *date* you. Cousin Flynn is in love with your boobs."

Flynn threw a pen at Logan. "Don't be a dick. Cora's got more going for her than just her boobs. Magnificent, by the way."

Cora blushed as Flynn winked and asked:

"Who's up for more Friendly Fire?"

Birdie suggested they go outside and pushed the button to open the sliding glass doors. Drake and Leo followed her onto the deck. She pointed up to the night sky filled with stars viewed through the opening in the tall trees. "Is that the north star?"

"I think that may be Venus," said Drake.

"What an amazing night," said Leo. "This house and property. I mean, you live and a god-damned fairyland."

Birdie said, "It's a rumor. There are no real fairies here. Only racoons, squirrels, and birds mostly."

Leo laughed. "Where I come from, there's nothing like this."

"Where do you come from?"

Leo, at six feet, looked down at Birdie who was five feet three. He tentatively touched her shoulder, as if in need of human contact, then let go. "You don't want to know."

"But I do," said Birdie.

"I lived in my car recently. This beat-up van. Did some couch surfing for awhile. Never anything permanent. Not the best views of the world." He was dismissive with a laugh. "It's all okay. I'm not complaining. That's life."

"Where did you grow up?"

"Central Valley. Lodi. Farming country. My dad grows almonds. Nice guy. My mom does lots of bake sales. Active in the community. I never really fit in. We're not estranged or anything. I call and write to them. We keep in touch. Well, now that I'm sober."

"You have a home here."

"Thanks, Birdie," said Leo. "Thoughtful. But I need the city. To play my music."

"You're super talented."

"You are," echoed Drake.

"Thanks. Your mom was a godsend. She saved me, really. I have her to thank for being here. All of this."

"I'm glad you're here, Leo. I didn't even *know* about you until you showed up today!"

"Yeah, well, I wasn't in the greatest shape for a time. It's better you didn't know I existed. Also, your dad's pretty cool."

"He is. And Sky, your mom, is too. Once you get to know her. She's talented like you. She's going to be a star. I predict you both will become stars. That's my Christmas wish."

Leo smiled and pulled Birdie into a shoulder hug. "Thanks."

The adults were gathered in the living room. Bill had provided after-dinner drinks. Iris had arranged the unwrapped assortment of gifts beneath the tree to appear more attractive, and finally took a seat herself. She sighed, expressing contentment.

Blaise sipped his White Russian and asked her, "Now that you fired Dad's caregiver for the holidays, what do you plan to do?"

"We'll manage," said Iris, "as we always do."

"Takes a helluva lot of work and expense to maintain this place and keep it up and running. Plus, taking care of Dad."

"What's your point, Blaise?"

"Have you considered putting the house on the market?"

"Never," said Iris. "Banish the thought."

"This place is worth millions. It'll pay off any debts you—"

"We're doing fine," said Bill. "Don't you worry."

Blaise stirred his cocktail. "Birdie sure is a curious little girl."

"She is," said Sky. "And I love that about her."

"Relentless too," added Blaise. "She and her friend, and now your son, who showed up, Sky, keep asking questions. They're on a quest to solve Mother's murder, along with those other four artists. It's starting to give me a headache."

Jess looked up from his mobile phone. "Why? Is there any new information that's come to light?"

"Not really," said Blaise. "They asked about her last paintings. They all have tally marks, apparently, which signifies I have no idea what. Oh, and that switchblade found with her body? They asked about that too, wanting to know what I knew about it."

"And?"

"Jess, I know as much as what those detectives know. Nothing. It's an unsolved mystery. I advised the kids to let the matter rest and try to enjoy Christmas."

"Did you tell them about the abandoned car?"

"Yes, Sky, I did. Which led us nowhere."

"Still, it's unsettling," said Iris. "The coincidence! I mean, the man who owned the car, just happened to be the father of our *nanny* who he transfered the car to. It was registered with the DMV in her name. When questioned by the police, she claimed she never owned the car. It had to have been stolen, she asserted."

Sky added, "Not only that, she passed a polygraph test when she was interrogated."

"Blaise," said Nora "you never told me you had a nanny."

"Her name was Lena," said Sky. "We loved her."

"We did," echoed Iris. "I never understood why she left."

"We grew up," said Blaise. "She wasn't needed anymore."

"No, Blaise," said Iris. "She was part of our family. Mom and Lena became very close, like sisters. That's what I remember."

"We sort of adopted her," Sky told Jess.

"Snow White was her nickname," Iris laughed fondly. "Because she was so pretty and looked like that cartoon character."

Nora asked, "This woman lived here with you?"

"Not in the beginning," Sky explained. "She was about nineteen when Mom and Dad hired her. Right?"

"Sounds right," said Blaise. "You girls were newborns and I was three. You don't remember much at that age."

Jess was now engaged, interest piqued. The movie he imagined this could become was reforming inside his head. "How long had she been your nanny?"

Sky and Iris looked at Blaise for assistance.

"Eight or nine years? She was twenty-seven when she left."

"Abruptly," said Sky. "It was a shock. She packed up and left without barely saying goodbye. It was not like her at all."

"I remember we cried for days," said Iris.

"We did," said Sky.

Jess asked, "What happened? Was she fired?"

"Mom and Dad never told us," said Iris. "It's not like we didn't ask. Mom was adamant, telling us, 'No more questions. Lena is gone and that's that. End of story.'"

Blaise sipped his drink, glanced at their father, wondering if he could hear their conversation as he sat in his wheelchair.

"What year did she leave?"

"Jess, darling," said Sky, "does it really matter?"

"Maybe. I'm curious to know."

"Let me think." Sky looked at Iris. "1991?"

"1992," said Blaise. "I was twelve."

"Wasn't that the same year your mother went mad?"

Ashwood was listening. He was paralyzed but he wasn't deaf. After losing the sensation of touch, his sense of hearing heightened. Their conversation was activating his sense of memory too. He knew exactly why Lena had left. It was no mystery to him and, even if he had the ability to speak, he still wouldn't tell them why.

Cassy had invited their nanny to move in with them and Lena eagerly accepted. She took over the guest room. At the time, Lena was twenty-five years old. She had few possessions to bring with her, so Cassy gave Lena a credit card to buy new clothing and furnish the room with a few accessories of her choosing. Ashwood was intrigued by the items she purchased. The queen-size bed was recovered with a rose-colored comforter and black-lace pillows. She placed bubbling blue-green lava lamps on each of her nightstands. Her walls were full of movie posters: *The Shining, Star Wars, Back to the Future, The Godfather, Dirty Dancing, Vendetta,* and *Aliens.* On the wall behind her headboard she installed a pink neon sign that glowed with the words: *Love Me.*

In addition to these new furnishings, Lena began wearing tight jeans, baggy linen pants, silk blouses, and cotton tops that revealed her belly button. Her personality hadn't changed; she maintained a sweet and virtuous demeanor. Nevertheless, there were glimpses of another Lena to emerge when she occasionally came home at night stinking of alcohol and sex. Awoken by a crash from downstairs one night, Ashwood went to investigate and found Lena lying on the floor. She was so drunk he helped her upstairs and onto her bed.

A year later, Ashwood had passed her bedroom, the door open, and glanced inside. He saw her naked.

"Oh," she gasped with embarrassment, covering herself.

Ashwood averted his eyes, dismissing the incident, the exposure, as an accident and not worth mentioning to Cassy. His mind began to change when he returned home late one night, climbed the stairs, and noticed Blaise leaving Lena's bedroom. To convince himself the visit had a logical explanation, Ashwood rationalized his son was asking her for private advice about an incident happening at school, or wanting her suggestions for talking to a girl – something he might be embarrassed to ask his mother. A number of things were possible, because Lena had become a part of the family and was like an older sister or aunt to Blaise.

Ashwood recalled hearing noises coming from Lena's bedroom and he stopped at her door to listen. When he recognized two voices, he opened the door and was shocked to find their nanny having sex with their twelve-year-old son.

Lena was dismissed and asked to leave.

ASHWOOD

CHAPTER 23

1988

Cassy was standing on a ladder, working on a large canvas nailed to the wall when Aaron entered.

"I have good news."

Cassy looked over her shoulder. "I'll be the judge of that."

"It's huge." Aaron glanced over at the day-care corner of the room and gave a wave to his kids and Lena. "Potentially huge."

"Are you going to tell me?"

"Art World Magazine wants to interview you."

"Shit."

"I know."

"Shit, meaning, I'm not good at giving interviews, Aaron."

"You'll be fine."

"That's what you told me about giving birth to twins." Cassy dabbed her paint brush into the puddle of oxide red. "And, if you recall, I almost died."

"You're not going to die."

"I have you to kill if I need to come back from the dead."

Aaron laughed. "So what should I tell them?"

"Fine. I'll do it. Are they coming here?"

"They want you to come there. It will also be televised."

"Fuck."

"You'll do fine."

"Stop saying that. You know I can't control my thoughts when I get nervous and feel pressured to say something intelligent."

"You're smarter than you think."

She laughed. "Don't make me fall off this ladder."

"Are you ever going to say why you keep avoiding your friends, the Gang of Five?"

"I'll tell you tonight over cocktails."

"Later then." Aaron turned to go, but turned back, captivated by the unfinished painting. "That's one powerful image, whatever it is you're creating. Wow. The emotion. That face. The blood. The tears. It's amazing. Do you have a name for it yet?"

"*Jesus Wept.*"

"Betrayal," said Cassy, pouring herself a glass of wine.

"I'll take some of that," said Aaron. "The wine, I mean. Are you saying they betrayed you?"

"That's what I'm saying." She handed him a glass of wine.

"All of them?"

"I don't know. I'm conflicted. I can't face them again."

"You haven't talked at all?"

"I sent them a thank-you card when I was laid up in bed after giving birth and almost died."

"Cassy, that was *five* years ago."

"I can count. I've sent them postcards showing photos of the Golden Gate Bridge, Mount Tamalpais, Muir Woods, and redwood trees. One had illustrated text saying, 'Greetings from Marin.'"

"Jesus, Cassy. These were your friends. We live less than an hour's drive away. On these cards, what did you write?"

Cassy opened the refrigerator. "Do you want some cheese?"

"Sure. Tell me."

"Oh, I don't know." She proceeded to cut some muenster cheese with a guillotine slicer. "Something like, 'I've missed you,' and 'I'll visit some day,' and 'Sorry, I don't know what to tell you right now.' That sort of message. Here."

"That's it?"

She slid over the plate of cheese. "I'll cut up an apple."

"Cassy, maybe it's none of my business but what the fuck are you keeping from me? What did they do to make you cut them off like that? Please, tell me."

She washed off an apple, removed a knife from its wood block, held it up for Aaron to see, then cut the apple in half. "Well, if you must know, Oscar, for one, lied to me. My supposed friends stole a hundred thousand dollars from me. Us. Victor, really."

"Are you saying—"

"Yes. The money that was meant to pay off drug dealers so they wouldn't kill us."

"How do you know this?"

"By accident. At a Gang of Five open house party I asked Oscar about Eric, if he'd seen him, wondering if he'd threaten us for more money. He brushed it off, saying he'd seen Eric in a bar, but didn't approach him, saying he thought it was over, yada-yada shit talk like that which was pure bullshit! I found out that same night that Eric had died of a heroin overdose shortly after he'd threatened us."

"You're kidding."

"I wish. Here." She placed the slices of apple on the plate with the cheese. "Now I'm thinking it was all a hoax. Not the part where we were threatened by Eric. But who knows? Maybe he was in on it too. I don't know what to believe anymore."

"Wasn't Oscar assaulted and stabbed with a knife?"

"Was he? I never saw proof. I only know for sure he lied to me. It was a blatant fucking lie! I thought we were friends. Friends don't do that. Fuck!"

Cassy collapsed on the kitchen stool, on the verge of tears.

"You think the others knew, and are complicit?"

Cassy drank some wine. "Just before I gave birth to Sky and Iris and nearly died, I overheard the four of them denigrating me and pretty much confirming what I feared. I heard Luca say, 'A hundred grand taken from a million is nothing.' Followed by Jimmy saying, 'she's still a rich bitch and none the wiser.' So, yeah, I'm pretty sure they all conspired to fuck me over."

"Jesus. I had no idea. That's unconscionable."

"I *know*. It'll kill me if it's true."

"Cassy, it's killing you already. You need to talk to them."

"No, I don't. I can't. I wouldn't know what to say."

"Do you want me to—"

"No. It's over. What's done is done."

"Cassy, I get it. Oscar lied. But maybe he—"

"The sickest part of all, Aaron, is that if he desperately needed the money, I swear to God, I would have given it to him. To all of them. As a loan, or a gift, or *whatever*. That's how much those guys meant to me. Fuck!"

"Cassy. What if you're wrong? What if the money actually did go to pay off some drug dealers? It's possible, right?"

"Then I'd have to kill myself out of shame."

Cassy was sitting in the green room, waiting to go on air to be interviewed for a popular network talk show that she never watched. She didn't watch talk shows or much television at all. She preferred to spend her time painting or playing with her kids. She was trying to calm her nerves by drinking the proffered alcohol while thinking what she would be asked and what she could possibly say about art that meant anything relevant to anyone.

Aaron entered the room. "They're almost ready for you."

"What if I'm not ready?"

"Hey, slow down on the wine."

"It helps me relax."

"You don't want to be too relaxed. Just be yourself."

"That's the *last* person I need to be," she joked nervously.

A woman opened the door and stuck in her head.

"We're on in ten minutes, Cassandra. Time to go."

"*Shit*," Cassy muttered to herself, then braved a smile.

She stood and followed the woman down a hallway and then to a place behind a curtain wall and heard her name being announced. She sucked in a breath, smiled, and walked onto the sound stage. She saw the empty chair meant for her, sat and crossed her legs, thinking she should have worn pants and not a short dress. The bright flood lights distracted her, causing her to squint as she peered into the dark rows that formed an audience.

"Good evening, everyone. I am your host, Blake Perkins, of Art World Magazine. We are honored to have as our guest, a rising star in the art world, Cassandra Crow. Welcome."

The applause caused her to smile and relax a bit.

"Thank you, Blake."

"Cassandra—"

"Call me Cassy."

"Cassy." The interviewer smiled. "You rarely give interviews so we thank you for coming.

"You're welcome."

"You've taken us all by surprise – bursting onto the art scene with your *incredible* paintings."

"Really, Blake? I think my art is very credible."

Perkins laughed along with the audience, causing her to feel at ease, buoyant, with the alcohol boosting her confidence.

"Touché. *Amazing*, is what I should have said."

"Thank you. What would you like to know?"

"So many things. But let's start with your technique. Were you formally trained?"

"No."

"There was no teacher who—"

"No. I quit high school during my sophomore year."

"Running away from home. To come here. Is that true?"

"True."

"Hard to believe. You're completely self-taught?"

"I've been drawing since I could hold a pencil. What can I say, Blake? I like to draw."

"Indeed. And *paint*. When did you begin oil painting?"

"At seventeen, when I could afford to buy the paraphernalia."

"While working at a thrift shop in Haight Ashbury?"

"That's correct."

"Remarkable. I admire you for that.'

"You shouldn't. In the beginning I stole what I could before I could buy what I needed. But to set the record straight, I've returned to the scene of my crimes and paid back the art stores tenfold."

"I'd call that admirable."

"Call it what you like. I was desperate at the time. And thankful I was able to make amends. I'm *not* condoning stealing."

"Indeed, no. Let's get back to your paintings."

Cassy was feeling a bit drunk, chastising herself for admitting in public, on air, during an interview, she had been a thief. What next, that she'd killed a man? She knew she needed to be careful what she said but knew she lacked control of her thoughts. The interview was going well. She was asked about her past and recent paintings, how she developed her unique style, and her future projects. Then she heard Perkins ask about the Gang of Five.

"What was it you wanted to know?"

"Are you still associated with the Gang of Five art gallery?"

"Um, not sure."

"You were one of the five founders. Correct?"

"Correct."

"It's been said you broke ties with them."

"Said by whom?"

"The other four in the group. The artist named Jimmy told me, and I quote, 'Cassy flew the coop for good, or for the *bad*. Take your pick. She was always flighty, that damned Crow.'"

Perkins looked from his notes to Cassy who looked frozen.

"Care to comment?"

"No."

"You weren't flighty?"

"No. I'm sure he meant it as a joke."

"It didn't sound like he was joking, frankly."

"Did he say I was a little *bitch* too?"

"He didn't mention it. What caused you to leave the group?"

"It's personal."

"You're still friends, and not rivals?"

"We were never rivals."

"Luca, who's known for his abstract art objects, said, I quote, 'Cassy thought she was better than the rest of us. A bit conceited and stuck up about her art. And, when she came into a load of money, it all went to her inflated head. She cut us loose. I say good riddance.' My gosh, that's rather harsh. Care to comment?"

Cassy was crushed by Luca's words and left speechless.

"The other two artists didn't have kind words to say either, I'm afraid. I can see by your reaction this is quite hurtful."

Cassy felt she'd been intentionally blindsided, also challenged, by both this male interviewer and her former colleagues. She steeled herself as her anger boiled over and burst from her.

"Yes, Blake, I do care to comment. I'd considered all four artists my friends. And I respected their version of art. Yes, theirs is much different from mine. Is it better? That's not for me to decide. Art is subjective. I merely do what I'm capable of creating. If your taste in art is celebrity portraits duplicated ad nauseam to be idolized like a sycophant; or making pseudo-political declarations by resurrecting pieces of junk in the name of culture; or dribbling paint like a toddler pissing on canvases for lack of having a vision; or spreading paint like stucco and mud on canvas because you can't draw worth a shit; well, that's for the viewer to decide for themselves what is good art and what is the best, as opposed to crap, don't you think?"

Perkins was taken aback. His smile returned for the viewers.

"We'll be back after a short commercial break."

He leaned over, whispering to Cassy. "For the record, there is no contest. You, my dear, are the superior artist. Good show."

Cassy groaned, "I totally blew it, didn't I?"

"I wouldn't go that far." Aaron glanced at her slumped body in the passenger seat as they drove back to Marin.

"How far would you go?"

"Most of the interview went well."

"Fuck. I hate these things."

"It's the price of fame."

"I don't want it."

"Too late for that. Your art is too important to be ignored."

"Says who? All I want is to paint, Aaron."

"Cassy, these interviews are needed."

"For who?"

"Your fans?"

"If I *had* any, I probably lost them after what I said during that interview. I came off as a raving bitch."

"You didn't."

"I said some bad things."

"Your comments were articulate."

"Like a heat-seeking missile. I was mean."

"Your so-called friends said some unkind things about you and I blame Perkins for ambushing you like that. But you retaliated and defended yourself. I was proud of you. Under fire, you didn't cave and rose to the challenge. You did what you had to do to survive and speak your mind. Don't beat yourself up. Be happy."

Cassy took her eyes off the road to regard him. "I don't deserve you. You're too good to me."

"That's because I love you unequivocally."

"Let's go home and fuck."

A month later, Aaron walked into Cassy's studio. He held in his hand the latest copy of Art World Magazine.

"Have you seen this?"

"Seen what?" Cassy stepped down from her ladder.

"A glowing review! You made the cover. And they're calling you the '*Queen of the Canvas.*' What do you think?"

"Seriously? Did they include the entire interview?"

She grabbed the magazine out of his hand.

Aaron said, "I told you. Wasn't all that stress worth it?"

"Shit!"

"I know."

"No! This is bad."

"Cassy, this is good. What's wrong?"

She went over to a table, picked up a postcard, and handed it to Aaron. "I guess you haven't seen this yet."

The front side of the card had a photo of San Francisco. Aaron turned it over and read the message:

YOU ARE FUCKING DEAD TO US, BITCH!

It was signed, 'Gang of Five, minus one.'

CHAPTER 24

2020

Ashwood saw his son turn his head to look at him. He closed his eyes, haunted by the past. Blaise had lost his virginity at the age of twelve by engaging in sex with their twenty-seven-year-old nanny. Cassy lost her temper over it, imagining this carnal act taking place, and initiated by someone she trusted and believed to be an intimate friend. The duplicity and breach of trust was one more blow to her mental state and sense of hope in the world. She'd confided in Lena, telling her secrets about herself, as one would to a beloved sister. A female sibling she never had. She cried off and on for weeks.

"Knock, knock, Grandpa."

Birdie was standing in front of him when he opened his eyes. She was there with Drake and Leo.

"I hope we're not disturbing you."

Ashwood shut his eyes to briefly indicate no.

"Can we ask you another question?"

Ashwood blinked.

"We were puzzled by the tarps found covering grandma's body. Does it make any sense to you?"

Ashwood shut his eyes.

"Why would someone go to the trouble of burying her, placing two tarps over her, then covering her with sand? It's weird, right?"

Ashwood blinked.

"This will sound weirder," said Drake. "We googled magicians who had buried themselves alive. Some survived, some didn't."

"It creeps me out," said Birdie, "but we think it's possible she was buried alive. It's crazy, I know, but what do you think?"

Ashwood shut his eyes and kept them closed.

"Grandpa, what's wrong?"

Ashwood had searched for answers when Cassy had gone mad, having told him she'd seen God. For a period of months she stopped painting. She stayed in bed and retreated into sleep, having dreams that woke her, sobbing into her pillow. She was barely functioning, so he contacted a psychiatrist for help. He felt guilty but deemed it a necessity to invade her privacy, looking through the desk in her art studio. In a file drawer he discovered one folder with copied articles about magicians and their famous stunts – sawing a woman in half, catching a fired bullet, levitation, and cheating death by being buried alive. The later stunt was all about Houdini who had himself buried beneath six feet of dirt. He almost died, yet managed to survive. She had highlighted this article and text where there was a description revealing the secrets about this stunt.

Were these articles, complete with illustrations, to collect ideas for future paintings? There were other files stuffed with photos and articles. However, this folder labeled "Death Defying Stunts" stood out from the rest. Yet he'd filed it away mentally, nearly forgotten, until her remains were discovered buried under the sand on a beach they'd walked on when they had first met.

There were so many unanswered questions. When he opened his eyes, he was staring at his daughter, Iris, who was crouched down to be eye level and close."

"Dad, are you all right?"

Ashwood blinked.

"Thank God! We were afraid you might have died."

Ashwood shut his eyes briefly.

Birdie laughed.

Sky asked, "What ever happened to Lena?"

"Hell if I know," said Blaise. "I don't really care."

Iris came back to sit next to Bill after checking on her father and overheard her sibling's comments. "I happened to bump into Lena a year or two ago. I almost didn't recognize her. The years haven't been kind to her from what I could tell."

"Why? Tell us what you know," said Sky. "She'd now be in her mid-fifties by my calculations."

"Well, yes," said Iris. "That's right. I had come out of the Book Depot, having finished a light lunch, and began walking home. I did almost bump into her because she'd walked out of a bar, that one on the corner of Throckmortan and Miller. She was drunk. Her black hair was long and streaked with grey, she was sickly pale, and her eyes were half closed but widened in surprise when she heard me call out her name."

"Did she recognize you?"

"No, Sky. She didn't have a clue who I was. Even when I told her my name, reminding her who I was. That she'd been our nanny. Her foggy recollection, when it occurred, produced a startled look of guilt and shame. I sensed she wanted to walk away after a curt hello and be gone. But I asked how she was, keeping her there."

"She sounds like an alcoholic," said Blaise. "How drunk?"

"Very. I offered to buy her a coffee so we could talk and catch up on life. She declined. What I could get out of her was that she was living in her family home, that decrepit one on the outskirts of town. Divorced, living alone. Both her parents dead. She came off bitter, and angry. When I mentioned Mother's name, she called her a cunt."

"No," said Sky. "They were so close."

"I said that too. She rebuffed me saying they were never close. She told me she was only hired to be a servant and treated, I quote, 'like dogshit.'"

"That is so not true." Sky, appalled, glanced at Jess.

"Also, she blames us for persecuting her family. For the police suspecting her father of being involved in Mother's death, badgering her widowed mother with questions. Harassing her too because the abandoned car found near the Oregon beach where Mother's body was found had been registered in *Lena's* name, by her father. She claimed she never owned the car. She spat on the ground before walking away. Then she stopped and turned back to ask something strange. I had no idea what she meant by it."

"What? Tell us," said Sky.

"It was about Blaise."

"Me?"

"She grinned and asked if you'd missed her, and had learned any new tricks. I was baffled by her question. It made no sense."

"She was obviously drunk," said Blaise.

"You don't know what she could have meant by that?"

"Iris, no idea. She sounds looney."

Jess was listening carefully. "You said she looked guilty."

"Yes, at first," said Iris. "She did."

"If she hated your mother," said Jess, "even calling her a cunt while knowing she was dead. Who knows, maybe this nanny, Lena, was the one involved in your mother's death somehow."

"She did leave us abruptly with no explanation," said Sky. "She and Mother must have had a nasty fight over something, bad enough to cause her to leave like that."

Jess said, "Bad enough to want her dead?"

Ashwood was tired of wondering how Cassy died or who killed her. He didn't want to think about it, but he couldn't help himself. He thought about her every day, trying to focus on the happy times but, inevitably, the sad ending to her life always came up. He had returned home one day and she was gone. When she didn't answer her phone or come home that evening he began to worry. The four artists who she'd formed the Gang of Five art gallery with had all been murdered. One after the other within a few months apart, each stabbed in the heart with a knife.

Cassy's murder was different. She went missing. Her car was in the garage. Her purse with keys and identification were left in their bedroom. Was she abducted? There was no sign of a forced entry or disturbance. Nothing stolen. And then there was the abandoned car left by the beach where she was found. Police records were able to trace ownership of the vehicle to the father of their former nanny, Lena. And why was the car left? How did the driver, if it was her abductor, leave? Was there another person involved with a second car which they used to drive away? And why that beach? Buried at the location he'd taken Cassy to when she was fifteen, a signifiant detail. How did the killer know about this place and what it meant? What other secrets, and to whom, had Cassy told about her past?

Was she killed with that knife? Or buried alive, as his granddaughter alluded? He didn't want to imagine the horror she must have suffered. The knife was positioned near her rib cage. At least, that was what the police determined after interviewing the boy who had discovered her skeletal remains while digging a hole in the sand. The remnants of two tarps were found over her body, covering a camping shovel, an empty bottle of vodka, and the switchblade.

Seven years Cassy's body lay there buried at that beach, close to the shoreline, where the tide washed over her, wave upon wave, then receded, day after day, smoothing the sand above her, and leaving no trace of a grave.

CHAPTER 25

1990

Lena was sitting in front of Cassy, also seated, helping to apply makeup in preparation for a photo shoot.

"I'm so jealous," said Lena.

"Don't be."

"TIME magazine, for God's sake! You're famous."

"I never wanted it," said Cassy, squirming as Lena brushed on green eyeshadow.

"That's silly. Who doesn't want to be famous? I do."

"Well," said Cassy, keeping her lids shut, "be happy that you lucked out by having the prettier face."

"That's not true. Hold still." Lene placed her hand on the top of Cassy's head. "I'm almost finished."

"And you're still young. Your artwork is showing real promise, Lena. I'm impressed."

"But I'll never be as good as you."

"Be yourself."

"I know," said Lena, "everyone else is taken. Oscar Wilde said that. But look what happened to him for *being* himself. Sentenced to prison for sodomizing with other men."

"Keep applying yourself and you'll be great."

"I should tweeze your eyebrows."

"No. We're done. Thanks for grooming me." She took hold of a hand mirror to examine herself. "Nice job. You're a pro."

"I'm here to please." Lena pushed away from Cassy on the stool and stood. "Now let's decide what you should wear for the photo shoot. Can I help dress you?"

"You're like the little sister I never had. Yes, help me."

✳

Cassy fanned herself with a magazine to keep from sweating and spoiling her makeup. She glanced at the lighting equipment as it was assembled around her – the large light boxes, the umbrellas, and foil reflectors. Behind her was a crew of assistants adjusting the lights. The photographer was a woman. She was dressed like a man, wearing slacks, a dress shirt with sleeves rolled up, a lose tie, a satin vest, and hair that was buzz cut. She kept sticking a light meter next to Cassy's face before returning to peer through her camera. Cassy wanted to call the whole thing off, but sat there waiting.

Aaron gave her an encouraging smile and wave from behind the photographer, staying clear of the equipment and electrical cords. He was standing next to Lena who waved too. The children were all at elementary school, Sky and Iris in second grade, and Blaise in fifth grade. She was glad they weren't present to cause more distractions. The invasion of people swarming around their house was disturbing enough. Aside from the formal portrait shots they wanted to take first in the living room, the photo session was to include additional shots with her in her art studio and elsewhere. Then afterward, she was to give a sit-down interview with a head writer for TIME.

Cassy made only one request upon agreeing to do an interview. The Gang of Five art studio was not to be mentioned. If it was asked, she told the writer she'd end the conversation. No questions came up about her former flatmates. She was relieved when it was over and all the people and equipment had been removed from the premises. Aaron had left to work in the city on completing a theatrical stage design. Cassy opened a bottle of wine to share with Lena before the children got home from school.

Lena made a toast. "To your success."

"And to yours," said Cassy, touching glasses and drank. "I'm so relieved that it's all over with."

"You should be happy."

"I am. All the fuss and attention over my art was so unexpected. It's gratifying but overwhelming and, in a way, embarrassing."

"Why would you feel embarrassed?"

"The recognition is appreciated but I don't want my art to seem like it's a competition. Like, wow, first place. I won."

"You *did* win. You'll be on the cover of TIME."

"It causes unwanted attention and makes people jealous."

"Like me?"

"I don't mean you."

"But I am jealous," laughed Lena. "Happy for you too."

"That's sweet. Thanks for all your help today."

"Of course." Lena sipped her wine. "This reluctance to have your art be critically acclaimed, does it have anything to do with the Gang of Five artists you used to be associated with?"

Cassy nodded and took a gulp of wine.

"Do you want to talk about it?"

Cassy shook her head.

"Okay. Touchy subject." Lena smiled and rotated her wine glass by twisting its stem. "I like what you said earlier about us being like sisters. I'm an only child. You, at least, had your brother."

"Victor was a wonderful brother to have growing up. He still is wonderful even though ... you know."

"I know, it's tragic. Very sad. But you have me now too."

Cassy placed her hand on Lena's. "Thanks again for everything. I couldn't have managed the kids without you all these years."

"Speaking of which. Blaise is sure growing up fast. He's going to be a heartbreaker, I predict."

"God, I hope not. Why do you say that?"

"He's a handsome lad. The girls will go gaga over him."

"I'm not looking forward to their puberty years."

"Was it tough on you too?"

"No, not particularly. Why? Was it for you?"

"The bleeding. It took me by surprise. No one warned me what to expect. It happened in the middle of class. A gusher. The boys laughed. It was extremely embarrassing."

"I'm sorry," said Cassy.

"I got over it. A rite of passage, huh? Anyway, having sex for the first time. That wasn't until I was twenty. How about you?"

Cassy considered changing the subject. "Fifteen."

"No! With who? Aaron?"

"I wish. We were tempted. He was nineteen when we met and, well, it could have ended badly if we'd gone all the way. We drove to this beach in Oregon, talked and kissed, and spent the night together in his station wagon. I only knew Aaron for one day, because I ran away from home shortly after. We didn't meet again until seven years later. It's a long story."

"Then who *did* you screw?"

Cassy laughed. "This guy who called himself Arrow. I met him the day I arrived in San Francisco. He got me high on LSD, invited me to live with a group of others in this house. I had no place to stay so I went along and, soon after, we fucked. Lost my virginity. End of story. Satisfied?"

"No," said Lena with a laugh. "Not *even*. I want to hear the long juicy story. About you and Aaron. That day you met and then happened to reconnect and fell in love all over again. Tell me."

So Cassy told Lena the details.

Cassy and Lena were finishing the last of the wine. Cassy looked at the time and saw it was approaching three in the afternoon.

"We'll need to pick up the kids soon," said Lena. "Shall we go there together?"

"Sure, why not." Cassy was exhausted after the photo shoot and interview, now feeling the effects of the two glasses of wine and more relaxed. "Is it okay if you drive?"

"On one condition."

Cassy grinned. "There's a condition?"

"I'm teasing."

"So what is it?"

"Please tell me what's troubling you about this Gang of Five art gallery. What happened? I want to help if I can."

"You can't. Nobody can."

"Tell me," said Lena. "You can trust me. We're sisters."

Cassy let her guard down, feeling the need to tell someone other than Aaron. Lena seemed to be the right person. They'd known each other for seven years and had become friends, if not sisters.

"I was lied to and betrayed by a close friend."

"In this Gang of Five?"

"Along with the other three who I believe were complicit."

"Complicit, how?"

"They cheated me out of a hundred thousand dollars. It wasn't even my money. It was Victor's. From the insurance settlement."

"What happened?"

Cassy told her about the ex-lover who'd become a junkie and wanted money because Gang of Five was a name he said he owned. "Death threats followed from drug dealers he owed money, wanting us to pay off his debt, followed by Oscar, one of the artists, being attacked because we hadn't paid them a hundred thousand dollars! Then Oscar got stabbed with a knife but survived."

"How bad was he injured?"

"That's the thing. The stabbing. It frightened me and compelled me to withdraw cash and pay them the money. Later, I discovered Oscar had lied to me. I was worried these drug dealer thugs would threaten us for more money. But Oscar told me he didn't think so because he'd seen Eric, my ex-*fucker,* in a bar who, by appearances, seemed to indicate we were in the clear. When, in fact, it was a lie. Eric had died shortly after he'd first threatened us for money."

"I'm not sure I understand."

"Lena, I don't think there was a credible death threat. I became suspicious when I discovered Eric had died and Oscar had lied to me. I wanted to believe I'd heard him wrong. A misunderstanding. Until, one day, I was nearby when Oscar was removing his overalls and his t-shirt lifted, exposing his belly. I saw no sign of a scar from any stab wound. There was nothing but smooth skin. Then, one day, I heard them talking shit about me, all four of them, pretty much confirming what I'd suspected. They'd all conspired to steal my money. That's when I snapped."

"And you felt sure you'd been deceived."

"Yes. One of the artists, Parker, had supposedly rushed Oscar to an emergency room to have the knife wound examined and then stitched up. Therefore, Parker had to have been complicit in the lie. And thinking back on how the other two artists, my so-called friends from the Gang of Five reacted, so casually, they had to have known. I felt like a fool. Their deceit emotionally gutted me."

"I can see why." Lena touched Cassy's hand. "But had you ever confronted them about this?"

"No. It was too upsetting. I was pregnant with twins. I still had my doubts until I overheard them talking in private, Luca saying, 'a hundred grand taken from a million is nothing.' Then I heard Jimmy saying, 'she's still a rich bitch and none the wiser.' This happened right before I gave birth and almost died. I was recovering and didn't have the strength or willpower to do or say anything about it."

"That was seven years ago, Cassy."

"I couldn't face them. I guess that makes me a coward."

CHAPTER 26

2020

The twins looked at each other and laughed infectiously as they shared a private joke without the need for words.

Jess looked at Sky and Iris with a curious smile. "What are you two laughing about?"

"Nothing," said Sky, holding a smile.

"Fun and silly memories," said Iris, "that's all."

Blaise returned from the bar holding two brandies. He handed one to Nora and sat beside her. "What's so damned funny?"

"Thinking about you," said Sky.

"Me?"

"Stinson Beach," said Iris. "We had some fun times there."

Blaise looked at Nora, Bill, and Jess. "I swear, growing up with twins was spooky. They can read each other's minds telepathically. Which left me the odd one out."

"You were always odd, Blaise," said Sky.

"Just imagine living with twins from *The Shining*."

Nora laughed. "I love it. Really?"

"No, you wouldn't," said Blaise. "Had you been me."

"Blaise," said Iris, "you're exaggerating. We weren't bad."

"I know what you're probably laughing about." Blaise sipped his brandy. "When we were kids, these evil twins snuck up from behind me at the beach and pantsed me."

"In front of Lena," laughed Sky.

"Blaise had the *hots* for our nanny," added Iris.

"It wasn't funny," said Blaise, grousing.

"It was adorable," said Sky.

"You were so shy," teased Iris. "What happened to that bashful boy, the big brother we once knew?"

"I grew up, unlike you two."

Iris and Sky glanced at each other and giggled like mischievous little sisters again.

*

Ashwood was listening. He recalled that particular day at the beach they were talking about. Cassy loved the ocean and they had made many trips to the beach over the years. Their children, when very young, played in the sand and chased the breaking waves. They had searched for shells and sand crabs. And as they grew older, there were beach balls, swim tubes, sand castles, and frisbees.

On an Indian summer, 1991, they'd come to Stinson Beach with the usual paraphernalia – picnic basket, towels, toys – all family members, plus one. The twins were eight, their son eleven, Cassy thirty-seven, and he was forty-two. At twenty-six, Lena was soon to turn twenty-seven, looking forward to celebrating her birthday. She was happy, looking sleek and sexy in a tiny white bikini, which she revealed when she stripped down out of her jeans and cotton top.

Ashwood noticed Cassy's reaction to Lena's scanty attire, the sting of envy at her youthful body. Cassy, too, wore a two-piece swimsuit. Her bikini was aqua green, less revealing, and included a gypsy sash tied around her waist to cover her cesarean scar. They had arrived close to noon. With blankets spread upon the sand, Cassy and Lena handed out the prepared sandwiches and drinks. Blaise had brought his prized yellow boom box radio with him. He found a station which was playing *Losing My Religion*.

"I love this song," said Lena. With youthful exuberance, she stood, playfully moving to the music, before plopping back down on the sand. "I love to dance. We should all get up and dance!"

Ashwood saw Cassy glance at him, squinting with a smile and shake of her head. Was Lena high on drugs or just life and the wine?

Both Sky and Iris laughed at Lena's little dance. Blaise silently ate his sandwich but was intently watching Lena, smiling shyly at her when she looked his way. They began putting away the remnants of lunch and Lena stood to announce, "Who want to play frisbee with me?"

"I do," said Sky.

"I do," echoed Iris.

Sky grabbed the frisbee and ran with Iris toward the ocean. Lena held out her hand to pull Blaise off the sand.

"Blaise, come on! Let's have some fun."

He shook his head obstinately. "I haven't finished eating."

"Okay, well come when you're done." Lena ran off to catch up with the girls.

Ashwood nudged Cassy to get her attention, and tilted his head at their son. Cassy's eyes widened, followed with a smile. Blaise had placed a paper plate over his lap, covering his swim trunks, but was unable to hide his sizable erection.

Cassy whispered, "Our boy is becoming a young man."

Ashwood wondered, was that day at the beach the beginning to an end? Things began to unravel within their family structure when he caught Lena having sex with their twelve-year-old son. Cassy had gone ballistic. The exchange between Cassy and Lena was a private conversation, ending in screams behind a closed door. What was said had to have been intense, vicious, and hurtful to both women.

Ashwood recalled Lena storming from their bedroom in tears. She threw her clothes and items into a suitcase, left a scribbled note for the kids to say she was sorry she had to leave, then left.

Another incident occurred at the beach that same day and came back to haunt Ashwood. By all accounts, it seemed like innocent fun. What many people did at the beach, so it meant nothing to him at the time. That is, to bury someone in the sand. Both daughters had refused to be covered in sand. So, too, did their son, who challenged Lena to be the victim when she had suggested the idea.

"Fine," she said. "Bury me!"

Ashwood had looked up from his book. Both he and Cassy were lying on towels. He'd been reading. Cassy was sunbathing. When he saw Blaise and the twins taking turns digging into the sand not too far away with a shovel, he become curious.

"Cassy? Where did that shovel come from?"

"What?" Her head rose off the towel. "Oh, that. From the back of our car. I brought it. It's that camping shovel I bought. Don't you remember? I thought it would come in handy some day. And look, it's being used. The kids are having fun."

Cassy laid back on the beach towel and closed her eyes.

Ashwood went back to reading, looking up from time to time to see them digging a hole in the sand. Blaise had taken possession of the shovel from his sisters who, he felt, by his and their reaction, they were ineffective at shoveling. Sky and Iris backed away from Blaise as he took over, working furiously, as if wanting to prove his vigor to their nanny who was standing and watching. Her back was facing Ashwood. Her hands were on her hips.

When Blaise finished digging a hole deep enough for Lena to lay down into, he stood back and grinned at her. This was when Sky and Iris snuck up from behind, pulling down his swim trunks, exposing his genitals. Ashwood watched as Lena raised a hand to her face in surprise at his son's expression of embarrassment, quickly pulling up his pants. He turned and lifted the shovel at his sisters.

"Blaise, stop!" shouted Lena. "It's okay. No harm was done. Nothing I haven't seen before. I'm ready for you to bury me."

As Lena slipped into the hole in the sand, Blaise said to Sky and Iris, "You're lucky I didn't kill you."

"She saw your *weenie*," said Sky. "It's no big deal."

"Kids," said Lena, "are you going to cover me or not? Play nice or I'm getting out of here now."

Ashwood watched as they proceeded to cover Lena with sand, her entire body, leaving only her head. His daughters were shrieking with laughter at the sight of their nanny buried up to her neck. This woke Cassy from her sleep. She lifted her head to see what all the commotion was about.

She gasped, "Kids, what have you done to Lena?"

"We buried her, Mommy. See?"

"How could you let them do that to you?"

"They're only having fun," said Lena. "It's okay."

Cassy shuddered. "Not for me. That's my worst nightmare. I'm claustrophobic. I'd freak out if someone ever did that to me." She lay back on the towel and shut her eyes.

Sky and Iris teased Lena, touching her nose, finding this funny then getting bored, standing and tossing the frisbee at one another. Blaise stayed on the sand, looking at Lena, who smiled.

"Now that you have me where you want, what do you plan to do with me, Blaise?"

CHAPTER 27

1992

It was a bad, turbulent year. The worst ever, almost.

A few days after New Year's Eve, Aaron arrived home late one night and heard unusual noise as he passed Lena's room in the hall. He stopped to listen, detected a male panting voice and opened the door, surprising himself and his twelve-year-old son who was having sex with their nanny. It was a shock, but more shocking was the manner in which the act of intercourse was being performed. Lena was naked, spread-eagled on the bed, with both wrists bound by handcuffs to the bed posts. Blaise, too, was naked, on his knees, between her legs, rocking back and forth as he penetrated her.

Aaron, stunned, didn't move and said nothing. It was Lena who then noticed him and let out a stifled yelp, because her mouth was gagged with a rubber ball attached to a head strap. Aaron could not process, or believe, what he was witnessing. Blaise thought her yelp was part of the game of sex they were playing and was oblivious that his father was at the door watching.

"Blaise, it's your father. Stop what you're doing."

His son turned, falling away from Lena. He slid off the bed and stood. It was the middle of the night. Aaron wondered how long this had been going on between them. He walked over to the bed to look down at Lena helplessly gagged and tied to the bed. He saw a set of keys on her nightstand.

"Are these to unlock the cuffs?"

Blaise nodded.

"You can go to your room now. I'll talk to you in the morning. I want to have a word with Lena. Go, damn it!"

Blaise left the room. Aaron picked up the keys to the handcuffs and held them in his fist, shaking his head, still in disbelief.

"Snow White, what have you done to yourself? Not so innocent anymore, I see. I should leave you like this until morning and have Cassy wake up to find you lying here. Or, I could unlock these cuffs and set you free. Would you prefer I do that?"

Lena muttered with the ball in her mouth, nodding her head.

"I'll take that as a yes."

Aaron unlocked one handcuff, moved to the other side of the bed and freed her other wrist. She pulled off the head strap and gag and started to speak. He held out his hand.

"Save it, Lena. There's nothing you can say that can make this right, acceptable, or turn back time. We'll talk in the morning."

Aaron knew this would devastate Cassy. Another betrayal from someone she'd considered a close friend, had confided in, telling her secrets, treating her as part of the family, and trusting her with their children. The girls were heartbroken, crying and demanding to know why Lena had left them abruptly, blaming their mother because she wouldn't tell them why. Cassy was generous and loving to a fault but would be mean when she felt betrayed, not holding back her vitriol. She burned bridges and made sure the relationship was irreparable. She punished Blaise by grounding him to prevent any social activities and told him she was ashamed of his deviant behavior.

In truth, she felt conflicted. She, herself, had been a wild child in her youth. Her children knew she had been a teenage runaway but didn't know the full extent of her promiscuous past. And Blaise was a pubescent male, sexually curious. It was natural for him to want to explore his hormonal desires. And if given the opportunity, which Lena provided, he would, and did, as she imagined she would have too had she been born a boy. Nevertheless, Blaise was grounded for a month and Lena remained persona non grata.

With Cassy's paintings becoming so popular and desired by art galleries, Aaron became her manager and agent, in addition to his regular work designing and overseeing the construction of stage sets for theater companies, and occasionally buying, upgrading, and then flipping houses for a profit. He hired a company to archive Cassy's paintings digitally and contacted collectors who had purchased her work to retrieve her images for posterity. Cassy left the business side of the art world to Aaron. She'd become more and more of a recluse, spending time in her art studio, rarely leaving their home, except for occasional gallery openings and private parties. She turned down most requested interviews, which had become tedious, overexposing her to redundant questions. Her social skills had improved. She was even enjoying the banter and chitchat when among fans and friends. No longer did she drink alcohol to excess, which caused her to speak unfiltered and offend people.

Aaron tried with no success to talk Cassy into coming with him to Ashland, Oregon. He was responsible for creating one of the set designs at the annual Shakespeare Festival. Their daughters were away at summer camp and their son was vacationing with a friend's family at Lake Tahoe. So the timing was perfect, but Cassy declined, wishing to stay home, paint, and relax in solitude. Aaron packed for the weekend trip, kissed her goodbye, promising to call her when he arrived in Ashland, and drove off in his new Peugeot 505.

He was disappointed that Cassy hadn't joined him, for he was hoping the trip to Oregon might rekindle found memories of when they first met. He enjoyed the five-and-a-half hour drive, giving him time to disengage from his normal hectic day-to-day pace and reflect on things he loved while listening to music. After checking into the hotel where he was staying, he called Cassy. She was relaxing outside on their deck with a glass of wine. She told him about the painting she had completed that afternoon. She described to him the image of an unformed half-woman, half-man, emerging from a cocoon, about to transform into a butterfly. She told him she loved him and that she was happy he called, then hung up.

The following day he'd been busy backstage, overseeing the set design, making adjustments to the transitions in the revolving stage, getting the mechanism to work as planned, and relieved when it did. After the matinee, during a break before the evening performance, he tried to call Cassy but she didn't answer the phone. He called again after the show but still no answer. After several tries with no success, he became worried, troubled with a premonition that something was horribly wrong.

He informed the theater company and his assistants he urgently needed to leave early for an emergency and would miss the Sunday matinee. Aaron arrived home late at night to find the world he had known and the wife he loved were irreparably changed.

Cassy was in her studio when the phone rang. Assuming it was Aaron who said he'd be calling around this time, she picked up the receiver and joked, "Stop harassing me, Aaron, I've missed you too." She was puzzled when there was no reply. "Hello? Aaron? I think we have a bad connection. Are you still in Oregon? Hello?" She heard breathing. "Who is this?" Next, she heard a dial tone. She hung up. "Fucking weirdos."

It was early evening when Cassy left her studio. She had always visited Victor, but he had died recently from organ failure. She was mourning his death. In the kitchen, she poured herself wine, kicked off her sandals, and walked into the living room – shocked to find Lena standing in the entryway. She nearly dropped her wine glass.

"What are you doing here? How did you get in?"

Lena held up keys. "An extra set. I came to return them."

"You could have mailed them or rang the doorbell."

"I was afraid you wouldn't let me in."

"You're right. What do you want?"

"To talk."

"I have nothing to say to you, Lena. Please leave."

"It's not that simple, Cassy. I have something important you'll want to hear. I can't change what occurred. But there's more."

"How do you mean, more?"

"Can we sit and talk? It won't take long. Then I'll go."

Cassy gulped down some wine. "Fine. Take a seat."

"Might I have a glass of wine too? To settle my nerves?"

Cassy considered telling her to fuck off and go but reconsidered, curious to know what was so important, and returned to the kitchen with Lena following behind. As Cassy set down her wine and turned away, Lena was quick to pour a vial of clear liquid into her glass. Cassy grabbed an empty wine glass off the shelf, removed a bottle of chardonnay from the refrigerator, and poured what little remained into the glass.

"Your keys," said Lena, setting them on the kitchen table.

At that moment, the phone rang. Cassy considered answering the call but became curious by Lena's frozen reaction to the ringing, as if she was a deer startled by the glare of headlights. Cassy picked up her glass and swallowed some of the wine.

"That would be Aaron calling from Oregon. He'll call back. I want to first hear what you have to say." With a hint of sarcasm, she said, "Don't be alarmed, Lena, there's more wine."

She returned to the refrigerator and removed another bottle of chardonnay. Opening a drawer to find the corkscrew, she proceeded to insert the device and twist out the cork as she studied Lena.

"You looked a bit startled. Why?"

"I'm fine," said Lena.

Cassy filled Lena's glass, then set the bottle on the counter. They walked into the living room and stood facing each other.

"Go ahead," said Cassy. "What's so important?"

"It's sad we ended on such bad terms."

Cassy acknowledged with a brusque nod and drank some wine, waiting for more to be said. "Continue."

"Again," said Lena, "I truly apologize for my bad behavior and breach of trust, the pain I caused, regarding your son."

"That's it?" Cassy gulped down more wine.

"No, there's more. But, Cassy, I know your past. You told me how promiscuous you were around that age yourself."

"I was fifteen, not twelve."

"With boys it's different. May I sit?"

Cassy gave a curt nod. "Don't get too comfortable. You won't be staying long." She drank more wine as she observed Lena taking her time, placing her leather purse alongside her on the loveseat, smoothing her short skirt, and then lifting her wine glass to her lips for a sip. "I was helping Blaise become a man."

Cassy scoffed and sat on the opposite loveseat. "You *fucked* a minor. My son! And more than once. I could have had you arrested for statutory rape. You're lucky I didn't press charges. If I had, you would have gone to prison."

Lena cradled her wine glass. "I loved your son. And—"

"Changed his diapers – when he was *three* – for God's sake!" She drank more wine to calm her nerves.

"I'm sorry I caused you pain. I love your family."

Cassy glared, emptying her glass with a quick swallow, then set it down hard on the table between them. "You crossed the line."

"But I didn't hurt Blaise. And, honestly, I'm glad it was me who he lost his virginity to." Lena sipped her wine. "That rite of passage is different for boys than for girls. The experience gave him more confidence for approaching girls."

"For thinking he can *fuck* them, you mean?"

"Well, no. An advanced maturity for when—"

"He ties women to bedposts?"

"What we did, they were only sex games. You must have known that Blaise was at an age where he was extremely curious about sex and eager to know what it was all about."

"Need I remind you, Snow White, you read Blaise storybooks when he was a child, tucking him into bed when Aaron and I were out for the evening. Ah, but, then he came of age, and outgrew these fairytales, and you felt it was your position, as his nanny, to provide him with advanced pop-up, x-rated versions. Is that your excuse?"

"Cassy, I caught Blaise sniffing my underwear when he thought I was away. If not with me, it was going to happen with someone. With me it was safe sex."

Cassy scoffed and stood. "You can go now, Lena."

"But there's still more to be said."

"Then get to the point." Cassy was feeling light-headed and sat back down. The room seemed to expand and brighten.

"Are you feeling alright?"

Cassy blinked, refocusing. Her senses were tingly and her body felt as if it was defying gravity, moving through space. She looked at Lena to ground herself. "Aside from you trying to justify having sex with my boy, what else do you have to say?"

Lena's cheshire-cat smile alarmed Cassy's senses.

"Why are you grinning like that?"

"You have visitors who will take it from here."

"Hello, wayward crow," said Jimmy's familiar voice.

Cassy looked over and saw the four Gang of Five artists in the entry coming toward her like strobed phantoms in a dream. She was not seeing clearly. The room was wavering in colors. She didn't ask how they got inside because she knew Lena was responsible for this somehow. She began to question if any of this was real.

"What's happening to me?"

"Same question we've been asking ourselves," said Luca.

"You slandered us, you little bitch," said Parker.

"Cutting us off," said Oscar, "for nine fucking years!"

"Lena, what did you do to me?"

"Lucy in the Sky with Diamonds. Remember her?"

"LSD? You dosed me. How much?"

"Hard to say," said Lena. "A lot. Enjoy the trip."

"Fuck! God damn you!"

She bolted from her chair, opened a drawer in an antique table, removing a switchblade and flicked forth the knife. Luca knocked it from her hands. He grabbed her by the shoulders, pulled her back, and pushed her down into the loveseat.

"Stay in your cockpit," he said. "We want answers."

"And retribution," added Jimmy.

Cassy scoffed. "Retribution? Fuck you! You all lied to me and stole my money!"

Oscar frowned. "What are you talking about?"

"Don't play dumb! One hundred thousand dollars! Remember? Yeah, that bogus pay-off to drug dealers!"

Lena faced Jimmy, "See, like I said," then she looked at Cassy. "I told them what you told me. I went to visit your former flatmates after you threw me out of your house. I told them everything. They doubted they could trust me. So I fucked Jimmy to convince him. Now we're lovers. And now they're here to fuck you."

Cassy heard laughter. She wasn't sure if it was coming from the herself or behind some hidden wall. All five of her intruders looked like badly-drawn cartoon characters. She laughed.

"What's so funny?"

"Nothing, Jimmy. Everything. You. Go away."

"We're here to stay," said Luca, lighting a cigarette.

"You can't smoke it here," said Cassy.

"Like hell I can't."

He tossed the burning match at her. She flinched at what looked like a shooting star landing on her. She screamed, brushing away the flame that landed on the floor.

"*Fuck*. What are you trying to do?"

Jimmy was back, standing before her holding a bottle. "Look what I found in the fidge. Champagne!"

Cassy watched with stunned sensations as he tore off the foil, tossing it at her, and then twisting off the cork. The *pop* sounded like an explosion, reverberating into the universe. Rain started falling. She felt the wetness on her face. The water tasted like wine.

"Time to party," said Parker.

"Yeah, Cassy," said Oscar. "What happened to all those wild parties you promised? You stopped inviting us."

Jimmy poured liquid from the bottle into a champagne glass and held it before Cassy. "Have some more truth serum."

She flailed her arm and knocked it out of his hand to the floor where it crashed to earth. "Fuck you all!"

"Now we're talking," said Luca, snickering, inhaling, blowing smoke at her. "I knew you'd want me sooner or later."

They were all hovered around her now, all five of them, with drinks in hand, looking down at her. She blinked, trying to focus, seeing more people hiding in corners of the room. She saw her mom and dad. Victor was in his wheelchair, helpless, unable to help her. Outside through the sliding glass doors she saw more movement and gasped, realizing it was her son.

"Let's play a little game," said Jimmy.

"Yes, let's," said Luca.

"In honor of our reigning queen," mocked Parker, toasting.

"To our flighty crow," said Oscar.

"Who flew the coop to fucking fame and fortune," said Jimmy. "Then shat all over us from high in the sky. Didn't you?"

Cassy rolled her head on the couch in denial. "Not true."

"Careful," said Parker. "What do we call the game?"

"Ah, yes," said Luca. "*Truth or Tear*. You're tagged, Cassy."

Jimmy drank, then placed fingers to his chin. "This is how the game works. We ask you a question and if you answer correctly, you receive a kiss. But if you don't, well, off goes a bit of your clothing. Ready? I'll go first. Tell the truth, Cassy, do you love my *Warholic* paintings? Celebrity portraits duplicated *ad nauseam*?"

Cassy was seeing devils and angels on the ceiling. "What?"

"A simply question," said Jimmy. "Do you admire my art?"

"Sure, Jimmy."

"Wrong answer!" Jimmy lunged forward to grab her blouse.

Cassy recoiled, "What are you doing?"

"Playing by the rules." Jimmy tugged, ripping buttons off and tearing the fabric apart until the blouse came off her body.

She screamed, "Stop it!" She tried to cover herself.

"I always admired your breasts," said Luca. "I wish you'd felt the same about my art. My turn. You liked *Perfidy*, right? And all my other pieces of junk created in the name of culture. My *crap*. Isn't that right?"

Cassy nodded, seeing double.

"Wrong!" Luca grabbed her by the ankles, nearly pulling her off the couch. "Parker and Oscar, hold her! Unbutton her pants." Luca proceeded to yank and removed her pleated trousers.

Cassy no longer struggled to resist. She had to believe this was not happening to her. It was happening to someone in an alternative world. She laughed at the absurdity of existence, then she realized it was she who was crying. "Why are you doing this to me?"

"You have to ask?" Parker said, "My turn. Do you like how I dribble paint like piss on canvases for lack of having a vision? Is that how you see my work, Cassy?"

She rocked her head, indicating *no*.

"Liar." Parker grabbed her ass and pulled off her underpants. "Now you've been exposed. No more lies. Your turn, Oscar."

"Nothing left to remove. Your scar, I see, is bigger than mine."

"What scar? You never had one!"

"Bullshit." Oscar lifted his t-shirt. "What's that?"

Cassy squinted, laughing at his fat belly. "I see a pregnant *whale* or balloon about to pop. Your skin is smooth as a baby's butt, Oscar. I see no fucking scar!"

"What do you think *that* is?" He pointed to his skin.

Cassy saw no sign of anything. "Nothing. You're nothing!"

Oscar sniffed. "Mud and stucco. That's what you said about my paintings in public, in print. I thought we were friends, Cassy."

"So did I. But you fucked me over and lied to me."

"When did I lie to you?" said Oscar.

Cassy was finding it hard to put words together, wondering if they were even coming from her. "What's his name. Carl. That one. Bass player. Remember him?"

"From the Gang of Five? The band. What about him?"

"He told me. The *truth*. Eric had OD'd. Years before you told me you'd seen him in a bar, telling me not to worry."

"What? That was a rumor. He *did* almost die. He overdosed, I don't know how many times, and did finally die. But not when Carl told you he did. Jesus, Cassy. You should have said something to me. Why didn't you? What's wrong with you?"

"So many things, Oscar. You didn't steal my money?"

"Maybe I did. Maybe I didn't. Who cares anymore? You threw us under the bus. You ruined our reputation during those interviews and made us into a joke, a laughing stock, while you were basking in all the adulation and glory of being famous!"

"As the '*Queen of the Canvas.*' What a joke," said Luca.

"The queen must learn to be humble before her subjects," said Jimmy. He tipped back his champagne, drinking the last drop, then set the glass on a table, and turned to Lena. She was holding two sets of handcuffs. "Lena is your replacement in the Gang of Five, Cassy. Your ex-nanny will assist me in administering your punishment."

Parker and Oscar held her body against the loveseat which had wood rails for armrests. She watched as Lena snapped handcuffs to both wrists at each end of the chair.

"What's going on?" Cassy was seeing ghosts crowding into the room to watch the entertainment. She saw a man with a mustache. It was the man who tried to rape her at a truck stop, whom she'd killed with a switchblade. He was snickering, leaning against a wall.

"As one who grew up in England," said Jimmy, stepping out of his jeans, folding them, before placing them on a chair, "I had always wondered what it'd be like to fuck the queen."

"Please, don't," said Cassy. She heard echoing laughter as she felt her body being penetrated. She shut her eyes, crying.

When she opened her eyes, Luca was grinning. "You were right about me. Spot on. So I borrowed one of Lizzy's toys. He held up a jar of honey. A bit of lubrication. Can you feel me now, bitch?"

Cassy felt something cold and hard enter her. She left her body. She was looking down upon herself. Her face was slapped. It forced her floating spirit to return. She opened her eyes and saw Parker now standing in front of her. He was unbuttoning his pants.

She groaned, defeated. "You're going to fuck me too?"

"Never would I sully myself and put my refined flesh into yours. Instead, I thought I'd create another masterpiece by *pissing* onto the queen's naked canvas."

Cassy felt the splattering liquid and realized he was urinating on her face and torso. Her tears kept coming. She blinked, shaking her head to clear her eyes. She saw the face of Oscar. "You too?"

"No. I would never touch or mess with this work of art. I only want to capture the memory on film for posterity." He proceeded to snap photos of her naked body with his camera. "Rest assured, these images will remain as our property, not for public viewing."

"Unless you tell anyone what transpired tonight," said Jimmy. "Reveal nothing. Like in Vegas. What happens at the Gang of Five, stays in the Gang of Five. Remember that, '*Queen of the Canvas.*' Take that as a warning. Parting advice to the now deposed."

As the four men receded from view, Cassy saw Lena at her side unlocking one handcuff. She walked around and removed the second handcuff, clutching them both to her chest. She looked down at Cassy and gave a tiny laugh, then a sad smile, mouthing, *Sorry*.

Cassy lay there nearly catatonic, staring at the cathedral ceiling as she watched the interplay of angels and demons. They looked like an arched mural in the Sistine Chapel, except they were alive. Most were oblivious to her presence while others were looking down, pointing and laughing. The inherent filters in her senses to protect her from seeing too much and going insane from the flood of stimuli entering her brain had been stripped away. She was seeing the world through a whole new dimension.

Eventually, not knowing how much time had passed, she forced herself to stand and came to the realization she was naked, sticky, and disgusting. She had been assaulted sexually and urinated upon. She walked toward the sliding glass doors and stepped on a shard of glass but kept moving as she bled. She struck the pedestal with her fist and the sliding glass doors opened with miraculous precision. She stepped outside onto the deck and looked up into the night sky, seeing stars through the aperture of the redwood trees. Gusts of wind made the surrounding foliage sway to the rhythm of clouds swirling overhead. Through the trees came the voices of spirits in sync with nature. Cassy saw the world as a finely tuned illusion, a never-ending engagement derived from God and His fallen angels.

She returned to the living room, shuffling across the floor. She stopped when she heard movement. It was a scurrying sound, as if someone or some phantom had lurched into hiding.

"Who's there?"

She waited but no one answered. It became quiet again.

"I know you're here. Leave me alone. Whatever you are."

In the darkness, she found her way to the stairs and clutched the banister for support. It helped guide her upstairs. She felt her way into the master bedroom and into the bathroom. Stepping into the shower, Cassy turned on the hot water. The liquid was scorching and she welcomed the pain, washing her clean, as she slid down the tile walls to the floor and began to sob.

CHAPTER 28

2020

Birdie, Drake, and Leo were seated in the library at the center of the room where there was a round glass table. They were looking through the art book titled *The Paintings of Cassandra Crow*.

"I've seen some of her art on the internet," said Leo. "I had no idea she was so prolific."

"Mom said she was fanatic about painting," said Birdie.

"No shit," said Drake.

"These are amazing." Leo flipped through the pages, stopping at a section titled, *The Dark Years: Heaven and Hell, 1992-1993*. "She painted only a few of paintings in two years?"

"The first one is beautiful," said Birdie. "I like how the woman, or man, is emerging from a cocoon to become a butterfly."

"Yeah," said Drake, "but these others are bleak."

"For sure," said Leo. "They lack color and warmth. There's no sense of life, or brightness. Dark and depressing."

"But good," said Drake, "I mean, in its execution."

"Execution is an apt word." Leo flipped the few pages back and forth to study the paintings. "She painted some weird stuff but, man, this stuff is disturbing. They're clearly about death."

Birdie said, "That's the period when Grandma Cassy had her mental breakdown."

"Yeah," said Leo, "I'm reading about it. "Damn. Do you know what happened to her?"

"1992 was the year when she told Grandpa she saw God."

"Your uncle said it was Hell she saw, not God."

Leo looked up from the book. "What uncle?"

"Uncle Blaise," said Birdie.

"How would he know what she saw?"

"Good question, Leo." Birdie took a closer look at the paintings from that period. "These do look like images of Hell."

"Yeah," said Drake, "for sure."

"Your uncle knows something about this," said Leo.

"That's what I said," said Drake.

"He may be only guessing," said Birdie.

"How old was he when your grandma—"

"She's *your* grandma too, Leo," said Birdie.

"Right. But when she went mad, how old was he?"

"You mean Uncle Blaise?" Birdie held up her fingers, counting. "He's forty, I think. So, 2020 minus 1992 is twenty-eight years. So that would—"

"Would make him twelve years old," said Drake.

"Interesting," said Leo.'

"Why?" Birdie said, "What are you thinking?"

"Birdie," said Leo, "Your uncle might have been there and seen whatever it was that happened to her. When she, you know, thought she had seen God."

"I asked Mom about it once," said Birdie. "She and Aunt Sky were away at summer camp. And Uncle Blaise was vacationing with a friend at Lake Tahoe."

"Oh," said Leo. "That rules out one idea I was thinking."

Birdie said, "What was your other idea?"

"You won't like it," said Leo. "It's probably not—"

"Tell us," said Drake.

"People said she went mad. I think she was literally mad. Angry and haunted by whatever she had experienced. These are images of death. Demons. Didn't she keep a switchblade in a drawer?"

"No way," said Drake. "Are you thinking she might have been the serial killer?"

"Hear me out," said Leo. "Was she ever considered a suspect? Questioned by the police? She broke ties with those artists and, what

I read, it wasn't a friendly break. There was malevolence."

"Are you forgetting," said Birdie, "she too was murdered?"

"But not like those other four."

"It still makes no sense," said Drake.

"I agree," said Birdie. "Grandma was a hippie from the sixties. She wasn't the type of person to kill someone with a knife. She was strange but peaceful, Mom said. So did Dad. Plus, she supported and donated to groups like Friends of the Earth and Greenpeace."

"Okay," said Leo, turning the page of the book to later years, pictures showing brighter images. "I'm only trying to help you solve these murders. Her death too."

"I know," said Birdie. "I'm glad you are."

"It's just..." Leo brushed back his long hair. "If the motive for those murders had to do with revenge then, well, all bets are off. It could be anyone. Someone you'd never suspect."

"Birdie," said Drake. "Remember, your cousin Cora mentioned revenge as a possible motive too."

"She did," said Birdie. "But revenge for what?"

Blaise was leaning against the bar, sipping more brandy.

"Brother," said Iris, "haven't you had enough? I noticed you've started to get a bit wobbly."

"Don't start on me, Sis," said Blaise. "It's Christmas."

"Yes, it is. And I'm glad you're together again with Nora."

"Me too. My fault. I can be an ass."

Iris laughed. "Yes, but you can be wonderful too."

"I don't know why she puts up with me and agreed to remarry. Love's a mystery. As is life. Skeletons everywhere."

Iris was puzzled. "Why? What's hiding in your closet?"

"Nothing. It's a figure of speech. I'm worried about Dad."

"So am I. He seems troubled. He's been crying a lot."

"Have you asked him why?"

Iris looked at Blaise with a frown. "*Yes* or *no* answers don't get me very far. And I'm not sure he'd tell me even if he could."

"It's about Mom, I'll bet."

"I'm sure you're right. Her death haunts me too."

Blaise downed his glass of brandy and poured a little more.

"Slow down," said Iris. "Are you okay to drive?"

"Nora is."

Iris saw her husband engaged in conversation with her brother's wife, being the gracious host and affable salesman, Bill had charmed Nora into a spontaneous and uncharacteristic burst of laughter.

Blaise said, "I couldn't cope being paralyzed. I'd want to die."

"You never know unless it's you. Life is precious."

Blaise scoffed. "You call that living? Have you asked Dad?"

"Asked him what?"

"If he'd rather be dead?"

Iris huffed. "Not that bluntly. But, yes. He shut his eyes."

"To say *no*." Blaise shook his head and looked across the room at their father. "I've been meaning to thank you and Bill for stepping in to take care of Dad. It's a burden, another one, I couldn't handle. I'm not much use with that kind of thing."

"It's what I do." Iris pointed. "Pour me some of that. Anyway, it's a privilege to look after Dad. And your financial help has been a welcome blessing, Blaise. Thank you."

He shrugged. "Least I could do. I wish I could have done more for Mom. If only I'd been older and not a god-damned coward."

"What are you talking about?"

"Nothing." Blaise drank more brandy. "I told Mom I'd always be there to protect her. I swore to her I would. I failed her."

"When was this?"

"As a kid. She told me how she'd been threatened when she was pregnant with me. Afraid she'd be knifed in the stomach like some artist friend of hers. She patted her belly and spoke to me in the womb, telling me not to worry, that she'd keep me safe. And, once born, growing older, I'd be there to protect her one day. She felt me kick her in the womb and it made her laugh, as if I was saying yes, answering her back, like a pledge. That's how the story went. She told me this when I was around nine. I swore to her, Iris, I *would* always be there to protect her. But I let her down."

"Blaise, are you crying?"

"No, I..." He wiped his eyes. "It's just, Iris, I—"

"It's okay to cry." Iris hugged her brother. "I haven't seen this side of you for a long time. I love you, Blaise. Always have."

"I love you too, Sis."

Sky saw Leo exit the library and pulled him aside to sit with him on the couch. They said nothing at first. Sky rubbed his thigh.

"I'm so proud of you for showing up announced. It was brave of you to call Iris and do that. I'm happy you did."

"Are you, Mom?"

"Very, but," she laughed, "at first, no. You shocked me. Now I am happy you did."

"That makes me happy too."

"There's so much I want to know about you."

"Not much to tell." Leo suddenly felt ill at ease. He looked over at the enormous Christmas tree, then back into the blue eyes of this gorgeous woman in her thirties, his mother, an actress, whom he had seen on video trailers for two years. And now she was before him, in real life, touching his leg affectionately. It was like he was starstruck. He sensed he didn't belong. He wondered if he should go.

"You play beautifully."

"What?"

"The guitar."

"Oh, yeah. Thanks. I'm trying to be good."

"You are." Sky touched his cheek. "My God, you're gorgeous. So handsome. The girls must adore you."

"Not really. I've been homeless, so—"

"Right." She dropped her hand, gave a laugh. "Well, Leo, you clean up well. And let's hope you stay sober. I'm proud of you for doing that too."

"I have your sister to thank."

"Do you hate me? Be honest," said Sky.

"What? No. Why would I hate you, Mom?"

"I gave you away when you were a baby to strangers."

"It's okay."

Leo touched her knee. Sky placed her hand over his.

"I want you to come and live with us."

"In LA?"

Sky waved Jess over and patted the cushion beside her. He came over and sat, nodding at Leo.

"I want my son, *our* son, to come live with us."

Jess blinked, surprised by the suggestion.

"Only if Leo wants to," said Sky. "Would you want that?"

"Um, I don't know. It's kinda sudden."

"Let Leo think on it Sky," said Jess.

"Los Angeles has plenty of music venues," added Sky, "and lots of opportunities. Live with us until you make it in the business. I'm sure you will. You're super talented. And Jess has contacts."

"I do?"

"Friends of *friends*. It's the perks of being famous. Say yes."

"I guess." Leo returned a hesitant smile. "Sure. Why not. If it's okay with you, Sir."

He looked at Jess who was slow to open his mouth.

"Jess will love you being there. We have a huge house. Plenty of rooms. Right, Jess?"

"Sure, Honey, if that's what you really want."

"Of course, I do. Oh, and guess what?"

Jess was afraid to ask. "What?"

"I want to get pregnant. I want to have a baby with you. I don't think it's too late. I'm only thirty-eight. And he or she will have a big brother. What do you say?"

"Uh," said Jess, stunned. "Wow. What's come over you Sky? I thought you said you didn't—"

"I did. I changed my mind. Say you want a baby too."

Jess smiled. "I do. But what about the pilot? Your career?"

"Oh, fuck that!" Sky laughed. "We'll make it work."

Jess laughed too. He looked at Leo. "Your mother, I have to say, Leo, is full of surprises. So beware."

"She's incredible," said Leo.

"That's an understatement." Jess leaned over and kissed Sky on the lips. He then extended his hand toward Leo to shake. "Well then, welcome home, Son."

ASHWOOD

CHAPTER 29

1993

Cassy refused to get out of bed. All she wanted to do was sleep. Her desire was to escape, to find peace and solace. Except she woke from her dreams sobbing. The first and second years following her mental breakdown were difficult, damaging the entire family. Aaron was at a loss as to what to do. He did his best to comfort her. He held her and rubbed her back, trying to coax out of her what had happened. She shook her head, refusing to talk. When she did talk, her words made little sense.

"God," Cassy answered him, muttering with her head buried into her pillow. "I saw *God*, Aaron."

"What does that mean, Cassy? You saw what?"

"Everything. Nothing."

Aaron kept sorting through the memory of returning home that night to find Cassy naked, staring into a mirror at herself and crying. He searched for clues in the items he found. The empty champagne bottle along with several glasses, five total, left on tables. Cigarette butts in ashtrays. Cassy's pleated pants, underwear, and torn blouse lying on the floor next to the couch. The loveseat had stains that smelled like piss. And the wood arms of the loveseat were scraped in places. Shards from a champagne glass were on the hardwood floor. And there were traces of blood footprints that led to the deck.

Aaron mentioned these things to Cassy but she acknowledged none of it, saying she remembered nothing. She refused to be taken to see a doctor, so he arranged to have one come to their home. As the doctor examined her, shining a light into her eyes, he noted what Aaron was concerned about. Her pupils of green irises were dilated. Her mind appeared vacuous as black holes in space.

"Your wife, I believe," stated the doctor, "has experienced some kind of trauma."

"There'd been people at our house, with her that night, when whatever it was happened to her. I don't know who these people were. She won't tell me, or she can't remember. She'd been mourning the death of her brother and told me she wanted solitude. But our living room showed signs of a party. A violent one. It didn't make any sense. Could her mental condition be drug related?"

"Difficult to say. Is your wife an habitual drug user?"

"Absolutely not," said Aaron. "When she was younger, she took drugs recreationally. But not anymore."

"I don't know what to prescribe for her, if anything."

"Will she recover from whatever this is?"

"Again, difficult to say. Time will tell. I'm sorry I can't be of more help, Mr. Crow."

"It's Ashwood," said Aaron. "Thank you for coming."

At the front door, the doctor said before he left, "You might consider having your wife see a psychiatrist. Call my office and I'll leave some recommendations with my secretary."

"Thanks." Aaron shut the door. He turned around to find his twin daughters standing beside one another in the entry.

"Daddy," said Sky, "will Mommy get better?"

Aaron fought back tears. "I honestly don't know, Sweetie. The doctor wasn't much help. But he'll be recommending other doctors who might be able to help her."

"I miss Mommy," said Iris. She held her sister's hand.

"So do I."

Aaron stepped forward and brought both daughters into a hug, rubbing their hair. He saw his thirteen-year-old son standing in the living room. After a growth spurt, he was now five-foot-six. He was idly kicking the wooden leg of the loveseat. Aaron walked into the living room with his daughters and said to Blaise, "Son, stop kicking the furniture. That chair did nothing wrong."

"Yes, it did," said Blaise.

"Blaise," said Aaron, "I'm upset too. I don't understand what happened to your mother. I'm trying to find answers."

"They wanted to destroy her! And they *did*."

"Who?"

"All of them."

"Who do you mean?"

Blaise looked at his father, then away, evasive with another kick to the loveseat before walking away. "Artists! Critics! People who hated her because she was more talented than they could ever be! Now she can't paint or do anything! And she's not even my mother anymore! I hate this fucking world! I hate everyone and everything!"

Aaron watched as Blaise ran up the stairs, then heard the door to his room slam shut. He looked down at his daughters who were both crying. He braced himself, fearing he might fall apart too.

Cassy was visited by a psychiatrist who had been recommended by the doctor. He pulled up a chair beside the king-size bed in which she was reclined against pillows.

"Ms. Crow, do you—"

"Cassy."

"Excuse me?"

"My name is Cassy. Who are you?"

"I'm Dr. Reynolds."

"Why are you here?"

"To help you if I can."

"You can't. I want to be left alone. Please go."

"Cassy," said Aaron, standing by the door, "Let Dr. Reynolds ask you a few questions. There's no harm in that."

"There might be." Cassy adjusted the pillows that she'd used to prop her up against the headboard. "Go ahead. Talk."

"Do you recall the night your husband returned home from a trip to Oregon and found you staring into a mirror."

"What about it?"

"You were naked, I was told. And crying. Why?"

"Because I was naked. Exposed for the world. And there was nothing left of me."

"Why would you say there was nothing left of you?"

"Have you ever been me?"

Dr. Reynolds adjusted his glasses. "Well, no. Do you know that would be humanly impossible?"

"Do I, Doctor? I believed a lot of things were impossible before that night when I saw God."

"Can you explain what you mean by that?"

"No," said Cassy. "God is inexplicable. Ask Aaron."

Dr. Reynolds glanced at Aaron who shrugged. "Many years ago when Cassy asked me what I thought God was, assuming there was one, I said God would be inexplicable."

"He was right."

Aaron added, "And Cassy, you said that if anyone saw God they would go insane because their mind would be blown apart, unable to handle the truth. Remember?"

Dr. Reynolds turned from Aaron to ask Cassy, "Is that an apt description of what happened to you?"

Cassy nodded and smoothed the bedspread over her legs.

"So God is inexplicable?" Dr. Reynolds cleared his throat then said, "But what about the people who were in the room with you on that particular night?"

"What people?"

"Those who you were drinking champagne with?"

"I didn't have any champagne."

"Well, then, the people who were drinking?"

"Apparitions. I didn't invite them. They came anyway."

"Did you know who they were?"

"Phantoms can't be known. Diabolical specters have no actual substance. These vile manifestations invaded my privacy and forced themselves upon me. And by doing so, their ungodly actions forced me to experience heaven and hell."

The doctor tutted to himself. "And see God?"

"It wasn't by choice." Cassy looked at Aaron. "Believe me."

Cassy's mental breakdown and sabbatical from performing any maternalistic duties resulted in their children assisting their father in the preparation of daily meals, specifically breakfasts, and dinners. They were given lunch money for school. Many of their meals were ordered by phone and delivered. Dining out at restaurants was not an option because Cassy refused to leave the house. Even if she had been inclined to dine out in public, her inability to function normally would have called unwanted attention and validate rumors that Cassandra Crow was afflicted with mental health issues.

The art galleries kept inquiring about paintings from Cassy, and Aaron made excuses for the delays in new artwork. Progressively, he was able to coax Cassy to get dressed and venture out beyond their bedroom and bathroom. They walked through their garden and sat on a stone bench beside the pond and trickling brook.

Aaron said, "I love you, Cassy. Thank you for coming outside. It's a beautiful day. What do you feel like doing?"

"Nothing." She picked up a pebble and tossed it at the stone statue of an angel. "I was happy once, wasn't I?"

"You were full of joy. And you will get there again."

"How?"

"Painting made you happy. Shall we visit your studio?"

"I have no reason to paint. I have nothing to say anymore."

"That can't be true."

"It's true. What is truth anyway? That word has lost all meaning to me." She gestured at their surroundings. "Beautiful. But is it real? Nothing feels real to me. We're living in an illusion, Aaron."

"Then let's make the most of this beautiful illusion, okay?"

Cassy smiled and rested her head upon Aaron's shoulder. "This feels good. But it can't last. Can it?"

He kissed her forehead. "If we live in the moment, Cassy. That's all we're given really. Let's make the most of what we have. Moment by moment."

"What would I paint? If I tried."

"Anything. Nothing. Whatever comes to mind."

"I'm afraid, Aaron."

"Cassy..." He caught himself from saying something stupid and meaningless, like *'there's nothing to be afraid of,'* because there were plenty of things to be afraid of. She had experienced something that scared the life and sense of hope out of her. He still had no idea what it was that damaged her. "I know you're scared. But I'll be right here with you. I'll always be here for you."

"Promise?"

"Yes, I promise."

Cassy stared at the blank canvas. "What do I do?"

"Draw or paint whatever you feel like. Experiment. It doesn't matter. Whatever comes to mind."

"Nothing comes to mind."

Aaron looked at the walls for inspiration. "What if..."

"What?"

"Maybe it's a bad idea."

"What? Tell me." Cassy swirled the colors on her palette into a grayish-brown mess.

"What if you tried painting what you experienced that night?"

"That's a terrible idea."

"Sorry. I'm only trying to help."

"I know." Cassy spread strokes of muddy gray onto the white canvas. "No, you're right. God damnit. It's catharsis. This is going to be hell. But I have to paint this out of my mind."

"Are you sure you want to do this?"

"No. I'm scared. But inspired. I have something I need to paint. And I'm going to paint the living *shit* out of it!"

Aaron stood back, observing her fury. She slashed the canvas as if the brush were a knife, and came close to knocking it off the easel. The undefined swirls of muddy color filled the entire canvas, then it began to take form as Cassy used smaller brushes, outlining shapes that appeared to Aaron as an interplay of angels and demons.

"Holy shit," said Aaron.

"You're a genius," said Cassy. She stood and wrapped her arms around him. "I love you, I love you, I love you!" She kissed him on the lips, then playfully brushed his nose with the paint brush, leaving a streak of gray. She laughed and sat back down on her stool to keep painting. "This is working. Thank you."

"You're welcome, I think."

Cassy handed him a rag doused with turpentine. He wiped the paint off his nose. "Do you have a name for this image?"

"'Holy Shit.'"

Cassy was improving day by day. Painting was her therapy. She spent most of her time now in her studio. She helped with the kids in the morning, seeing them off to school, and joining everyone for dinner. Still, she was not functioning with all mental synapses firing as they had before she'd been traumatized. Sporadic bursts of joyous laughter mixed with periods of despondent retreats into solitude. The family adapted to these mercurial changes in Cassy's personality. She destroyed most of the paintings she created, saving only a few, but she didn't care. The self-healing process of doing art was having positive results. She was regaining her confidence and enjoying the act of painting again.

After two years of self-imposed isolation, Cassy agreed to go out to dinner at a restaurant. Not used to the buzz of activity and noise created from crowds of people, Cassy felt she'd entered a hive of bees while peaking on psychedelics. She had trouble adjusting and was on the verge of a panic attack.

Iris was observing her closely. "What's wrong, Mom?"

"These people," she laughed. "So many. I'm fine."

The receptionist returned to her station to greet them as they entered. "Hi, I'm Jennifer. Welcome."

"I made reservations," said Aaron. "Ashwood. A party of five. I requested a booth in the back, if it's available."

"Yes, follow me. Wait." She turned and stopped them. "Aren't you Cassandra Crow?"

Cassy was a bit startled and smiled. "I believe I still am."

"I love your paintings. I'm a fan. Sorry. Forgive me."

"For what? Thank you," said Cassy. "It's nice to hear. That's kind of you to say. Our table?"

"Yes, this way."

Cassy and Aaron entered the booth first, sliding upon the vinyl seating to the wall, facing each other across the table. Sky and Iris sat on their father's side, Blaise sat next to their mother.

"It's nice to get out," said Aaron. "Not so bad, right?"

Cassy nodded and looked down at her menu.

Sky was enjoying the attention their table was receiving, smiling back at the roving eyes. "See, Mom? You're still famous."

"And loved," said Iris. "Thanks for being our mom."

Cassy looked up at her with a smile.

"I plan to be famous too," said Sky, sipping water.

"For what?" Blaise broke off a piece of sourdough bread.

"Acting." Sky brushed back her hair. "Being a movie star."

Blaise laughed. "You can't act. Try acting like a little sister and not a stuck-up little drama-queen bitch."

"*Blaise*," said Aaron. "Act civil. Social manners?"

"Is that our family motto?" He mocked, smiling. "Act happy? We should all win Oscars for *this* family performance."

Cassy's eyes were downcast, as if studying her menu. She had no appetite. She lifted her head and held her breath. "Blaise, your dad told me you signed up to play football at school."

"Huh? Yeah, I did. I figured, why not?"

"Good for you," said Cassy.

"I signed the school releases," said Aaron. "All the legal stuff. He needs a mouth guard. I scheduled a dental appointment."

Cassy turned her head to look at her son. "You've grown up so fast. Already a freshman in high school. How tall are you now?"

"Five-eleven. I'm surprised you even care."

"Blaise," said Aaron.

"Don't be a dick," said Sky. "Mom's trying hard."

"I am," said Cassy. "I'm sorry for being absent so long."

"We forgive you, Mom," said Iris.

"Okay," said Cassy, smiling at them all. "So, Blaise wants to be a football star. What do you girls want to be?"

"A veterinarian," said Iris. "Working with animals."

"I can see that," said Cassy.

Sky struck a pose and giggled. "You already know what I want to be, Mom. A movie star. I want to be famous like you."

Cassy saw a man moving fast toward their table, alarming her until she realized it was their waiter. "Fame comes with a high price, Sky. But, yes, I can see you soaring to great heights."

"Sorry, folks. Busy night." Their waiter was a young man who noticed Sky immediately, smiling back. "What can I get you? Does everyone know what they want?"

"Happiness," said Cassy.

CHAPTER 30

2020

Ashwood watched his family mingling in the living room. Most everyone had regathered by the Christmas tree. He noticed that Cora and Flynn, his niece and nephew, were absent. Blaise appeared to be clearly drunk, staggering, corralled by his sisters, Sky and Iris, who moved him to sit on the couch. He glimpsed a presence of something on his body. Noodle's furry face rose into view, becoming eye-to-eye with his. Its green irises looked alien. Its elongated pupils narrowed, staring into his, curious beyond words, as if the cat were trying to convey a message from another planet.

"Noodles!"

Birdie appeared and plucked the cat off him. She bent down as she held Noodles close, both faces peering at him until the cat bolted from her arms. She giggled.

"Did Noodles wish you a Merry Christmas?"

Ashwood blinked.

"Mom's trying to talk Uncle Blaise and his family into staying overnight. He's sorta drunk. We, meaning our team finding answers to Grandma's murder, wanted to ask him another question, but now doesn't seem to be a good time."

Ashwood shut his eyes.

"That's what I thought. You agree, right?"

Ashwood blinked.

"Did you hear that Aunt Sky and Uncle Jess invited Leo to come live with them in LA?"

Ashwood shut his eyes.

"They did. Isn't that cool? Amazing, right?"

Ashwood blinked.

"I love Christmas. All the unexpected gifts. It's exciting. Did you and Grandma love Christmas too?"

Ashwood blinked. Then he closed his eyes. They remained shut to summon the onrush of memories.

"Grandpa? Are you okay? Do you want to rest?"

Cassy loved Christmas. She made a fuss over the holiday every year and he loved her for it. When their kids were small she'd assign fun tasks for them to do. They created homemade paper ornaments for the tree. Wreaths and garlands were made from garden cuttings and plucked from branches in the forest, strung together to be hung throughout the house. Victor enjoyed participating with the children – Lena helping them all – in the stringing of pine boughs and cones together. They were united as a family, creating cards with paintings and drawings to send out to friends, including letters to Santa.

As their children grew, the activities expanded into baking and building gingerbread houses, creating unique ornaments from spools of thread, seashells, and ordinary objects, made special by the use of their imaginations. These holiday traditions remained until their kids reached the ages of nine and twelve. That was when Cassy lost her mind and the fun-filled activities ended.

Ashwood was puzzled by the loss. Over time, Cassy regained a good portion of her lost self, but never the full thrust of enthusiasm she'd once had for life. It was disheartening. Her children suffered in those years of their adolescent growth. Blaise took his aggression out while playing football. His prowess earned him a college scholarship at UC Berkeley, which he squandered inexplicably, dropping out of school after his sophomore year, drinking himself to excess in night clubs and sleeping with as many women as humanly possible. Sky was voted homecoming princess her freshman year, became a cheerleader, was prom queen her senior year, and became pregnant before graduation. Iris grew to be the shy, smart sister who studied hard, was also pretty, but was overshadowed by her twin. She graduated with honors but abandoned her dreams of college to attend to her bereft sister, consoling her during the nine months of bringing a fetus to term, and being with her as she gave birth.

It was all a mystery. Before Blaise went off the rails and Sky had become pregnant, Ashwood thought the worst was over and life had gone back on track, running smoothly again. Cassy was painting with exuberance once more. Exotic images emerged from her mind to be transposed onto canvas after canvas. Creations both whimsical and sublime. She'd painted transparent lovers kissing, embraced on a park bench with leaves and cherry blossoms swirling through their entwined translucent bodies. Another painting showed the backside of a naked man, standing with a camera to his face, photographing a woman with the hint of a smile while dressed in regal attire.

Interpretations of the human condition – scrutinizing reality – were the themes Cassy sought to portray. From memory, she had painted a portrait of Lizzy, whom she'd been fond of. Liz would pose for Luca while seated on a box, completely naked except for a wide-brimmed hat, her legs crossed and smoking a cigarette, emanating a defiant attitude. Ashwood marveled at Cassy's ability to capture the essence of people through her paintings. He was encouraged to see Cassy showing signs of being happy and optimistic again.

Then people started to die. People they knew. All four artists from the Gang of Five stabbed with a knife, one after the other, over a period of nine months. The change in Cassy became apparent. She feared for her life. As if sensing her time was running out, she began painting furiously. She dismissed the notion she could be next by this serial killer, but Ashwood could tell she was scared.

The cause of Cassy's death remained a mystery. But Ashwood had begun to have suspicions. It began when he ran into a friend of Blaise's. The year was 2018, two months before he'd had his stroke. The boy was now a man, same age as his son, thirty-eight. His name was Jason. The boys had been best friends during their adolescent years. They'd gone on family vacations together. Jason recognized Ashwood having dinner by himself at a restaurant in Mill Valley and approached him to say hello. After pleasantries were exchanged, Jason expressed condolences about Ashwood's wife – her discovered body seven years after she'd gone missing.

Ashwood told Jason he'd regretted leaving Cassy one weekend because it was the time she had her mental breakdown caused by some violent incident and there had been no one there to protect her. In hindsight, he wished Blaise hadn't been away in Lake Tahoe with Jason and his family. At that, a strange look came over Jason's face, who asked to be reminded of the year of that summer vacation.

"We left early that weekend," said Jason.

"How do you mean?"

"My dad had a business emergency and we returned Saturday, early that evening, dropping Blaise off at your house."

"That's impossible."

"No. That's what happened. I clearly remember."

Then where was Blaise? Ashwood had to wonder if there was a mistake, a flaw in Jason's memory, or something his son was hiding. Before Ashwood had a chance to confront Blaise with questions, he had a massive stroke. Now he was incapable of asking him anything. Paralyzed in his wheelchair, he watched his inebriated son seated on the couch between his twin daughters. Ashwood couldn't tell what was being said but his son's countenance was reeking of inebriation, guilt, and regret. He wished he had the ability to read lips.

The day after Ashwood returned home, finding Cassy standing naked in front of a mirror, Blaise showed up holding his overnight bag. He looked sleep-deprived and disheveled, like someone who'd slept outdoors in his clothes. Ashwood recalled Blaise saying little and avoiding eye contact as they cleaned up the mess left in the living room. His son showed a lack of interest in discussing what might have transpired the night before or the cause of his mother's agitated state of mind. Ashwood was still troubled by the memory.

"Grandpa? Knock, knock."

Ashwood heard Birdie's voice and opened his eyes. At first, he saw Cassy. She was smiling. She had come back. Then she was gone. His granddaughter was there, in her place, beaming with life.

"Guess what? Uncle Blaise and his family are going to stay over tonight. I'm sharing my room with Cora. Logan and Leo will stay in Flynn's room. We have inflatable mattresses, so it will all work out. Uncle Blaise and Aunt Nora will be sleeping in Grandma's art studio which has a roll-out sofa bed. Pretty neat, huh?"

Ashwood blinked.

"Except I don't know where Cora went. I need to tell her she's staying over and sleeping with me. My pajamas won't fit her though. She'll have to borrow something from Mom. Wait. There she is!"

Ashwood watched Birdie run off to meet Cora who had entered the living room with Flynn. Birdie's enthusiasm didn't transfer to the older cousin, who looked miffed. She was indicating her formal dress. Ashwood noted Cora adjusting the bust line, making sure her breasts were covered and not exposed. While talking to Birdie, she rubbed her lips a couple times, self-conscious about something, as her eyes stayed on Flynn walking away from her. Ashwood sensed something had transpired between the cousins. Something sexual. To what extent, he wasn't sure he wanted to know.

His eyesight moved to view Cassy's painting over the fireplace.

A radiant angel rising from the ashes. It was the last work of art she had created, completed several days before her disappearance. When he'd asked, she told him it was called *Afterlife*. One of the last words he heard her say before she went missing. Seven years later, Cassy's remains were discovered on a beach and Birdie was born.

CHAPTER 31

1997

Cassy's forty-fifth birthday was celebrated at home surrounded by family. Aaron was forty-nine, Blaise seventeen, and the twins had turned fifteen. Aaron, with the girls, had selected a three-layered vanilla cream-filled cake with chocolate frosting designed by a local bakery. It had the word "LOVE" written in pink on top.

Sky told her, "You only get one candle Mom because we didn't want to start a fire."

"Ha-ha," said Cassy, blowing out the tiny flame.

"What's your wish? Tell us, Mom," said Iris.

"No," said Cassy

"To be young again," said Blaise, "I'll bet."

"I've never been old." Cassy removed the candle and licked the frosting off the end. "Never as old as you, Blaise. God, you've grown into a giant"

"I'm only six-two."

"To me you're gigantic. And a football star!"

"Not quite."

"Your abilities earned you a scholarship to CAL," said Aaron, cutting the cake. "I'd call that stellar."

"Sky was voted homecoming princess," said Iris.

"*Jesus,*" said Blaise. "How many times do we have to hear that Sky is a princess. Congratulations. It's official."

"Thanks," said Sky.

"I was being facetious, Sis."

"Play nice." Cassy received a slice of cake. "Thank you."

Blaise took the plate of cake passed to him from his father. "Do you want me to make you young again, Mom?"

"I see no magic wand," said Cassy.

"You have to close your eyes," said Blaise.

"Why?"

"Trust me," said Blaise. "Think of an age you'd like to be and then shut your eyes. It's magic. I'll guess your number."

"How? Fine." Cassy closed her eyes. "I'll play along."

Blaise stood, scooping cake in his hand. "Mom, the number you should be thinking is *eleven*." He smeared the cake in her face.

Cassy screamed, shocked, rising to her feet.

Aaron shouted, "Blaise!"

"What?" Blaise laughed defensively. "She did the same to me on her birthday when I was eleven. Don't you remember, Mom?"

Cassy, not laughing or smiling, wiped the cake off her face with her napkin and walked off into the kitchen.

Blaise said, "Mom? Come on! It was meant as a joke!"

She returned with a hand behind her back. She approached her son who was still standing.

"Mom, I'm sorry."

"For what?" She raised a can of whipped cream, spraying Blaise is the face, laughing. "Nice trick! It worked! I'm eleven!"

Cassy entered the dining room for an evening dinner. Aaron had ordered Chinese takeout to have delivered. Sky and Iris were setting the table with plates, napkins, chopsticks, glasses of water, and a few serving spoons. Aaron was standing, uncorking a bottle of zinfandel wine. Blaise was already seated reading a paperback. Cassy noticed the title, another sci-fi novel about an invasion of something. She got everyone's attention by slapping down a magazine on the table.

"I received the latest copy of *Art World Magazine*."

Blaise took his eyes off his book. "*Fuck*. The Gang of Five made the cover? Fuck them."

Aaron was surprised by his son's vitriol.

"My sentiments too," said Cassy.

Aaron poured Cassy some wine, a glass for himself, then picked up the magazine. He flipped to the cover article. He shook his head as he read. "When did Lena become part of the Gang of Five?"

"I thought you knew," said Cassy.

"Sorry, no." Aaron set the magazine down and picked up his glass of wine. "When you cut them off and lost touch with them, so did I. Well, I guess they're finally getting their due."

"They'll be getting their *due*," said Blaise. "You wait."

Aaron looked at their scowling son as he focused back onto the pages of his book. "Meaning, what?"

"Meaning nothing," said Blaise.

Aaron asked Cassy, "Have you talked to any of them at all?"

The doorbell rang.

"Food!" Sky and Iris ran to the front door.

"They're dead to me," said Cassy. "No."

Aaron raised his glass. "I wouldn't let this article bother you. You are still the 'Queen of the Canvas.'"

Cassy flinched, drinking wine. "Please don't call me that."

"It's a badge of honor," Aaron countered.

"The magazine's good intentions turned me into a target."

The twins ran back in the room carrying bags. They removed the containers of food and placed them at the center of the table.

"A target for what?"

"Let's focus on eating." Cassy took a seat.

"Mom?" Blaise tossed his book on an empty chair.

"Yes, Blaise. What?"

"I'm going to make you proud of me one day."

"I'm already proud of you."

"No, you'll see, Mom."

"See what? You're sounding very *ominous*. Isn't he?"

"It's from reading all those creepy novels," said Sky.

Iris giggled. "He's our space cadet brother."

"Piss off," said Blaise. "I'm serious."

"Language," warned Aaron.

"You *sound* serious," said Cassy.

"I am. And I owe you. I won't ever fail you again, Mom."

"Blaise," said Aaron, "what are you talking about?"

"This is between Mom and me."

"*Ooh*, it's a secret," laughed Sky. "Whatever. Let's eat."

They passed around the containers, removing spring rolls and scooping onto their plates chow mein, sweet and sour pork, chicken fried rice, and cashew chicken. Blaise gritted his teeth as he stared at his plate of food. "I would like some wine too, please."

Aaron looked at Cassy. "Sure. A little for dinner. We know you drink on the weekends with your friends. Just don't overdo it."

Aaron poured his son a glass of the wine.

"Wine tastes vile," said Sky. "None for me."

"Yuck," said Iris. "Me neither."

"Thanks, Dad." Blaise raised his glass in a toast. "Here's to Mom. The greatest mother in the world."

Everyone lifted their glasses and drank.

"That's so sweet, Blaise."

"You'll know when it happens."

"You're being mysterious again. When what happens?"

"When you'll be proud of me, Mom."

Cassy was seated in a courtroom next to Blaise, waiting for the judge to call her son's name. He'd been arrested for stealing a flask-size bottle of vodka at a grocery store. He'd been taken away in a police car and jailed but then released to his parents since he was still a juvenile, under the age of eighteen.

"Is this how you planned to make me proud of you?"

"No." Blaise touched his tie, wanting to loosen the tight noose around his neck. He'd been forced to wear a sports jacket and dress pants. "I'm sorry, Mom, for putting you through all this. But, you know, it's not like you never did anything like this."

She raised her head to look up at her son.

"When you were my age, you stole stuff. I read that interview you gave in some art magazine."

"I stole food to eat, so I wouldn't starve. You stole liquor only to get drunk."

"You also lifted art supplies. You were just lucky you never got caught. Like Jason. He got away undetected. But I was the one who got nabbed. Luck. That's all I'm saying."

"You made your point. I'm a poor excuse for a mother. A bad influence on you."

"Don't say that," said Blaise. "You're not."

Cassy smiled and rubbed his knee. "You look nice all dressed up for a change."

"It was Dad's idea. To make a good impression. This isn't me. And the judge will know I'm faking it."

"No, he won't. You're a good-looking boy. Big and tall. Huge. I can't believe you came out of me. Let's hope this doesn't cancel your football scholarship."

"I don't really care about going to college."

"You should."

"I guess I inherited my renegade behavior from you?"

"I suppose you did. We're alike. It's my fault."

"Mom?"

"What?"

"It's not. And I'm sorry I failed you."

"You never failed me."

"I did. I promised I'd protect you. But I didn't when you really needed me. I was a coward."

Cassy frowned at Blaise curiously. Something unspoken passed between them. Before she could ask what exactly he meant by that remark, the judge called Blaise's name.

"I'll make it up to you someday, Mom. I promise."

Blaise was contrite as he stood before the judge.

Because this was a first time offense and he was a minor, the judge placed him on probation until he turned eighteen. His arrest for shoplifting would be expunged from his record if he managed to stay out of trouble. However, the judge warned, if he was arrested again, even cited for a speeding violation in a motor vehicle, he'd be placed in a juvenile detention center.

CHAPTER 32

2020

Ashwood was feeling weary. He saw the colorful angel rising, seemingly in motion, luring him toward her. Was it Cassy? He closed his eyes. His body remained at rest, paralyzed, incapable of motion, while his mind swirled like the wind inside an empty conch shell. He felt like the ghost of a spineless sea creature, a snail, with a brain. An awareness. With memories. But what good was it to him now?

Once upon a time, a fifteen-year-old girl stole his heart. He was love-struck. Then she ran away and he feared he would never see her again. But she reappeared, as in a dream. His life was given meaning. Like a fantasy become real. Real happiness. Real sorrow. Laughter and tears. All interchangeable. Unavoidable. That was life. But he wanted answers. Not the inexplicable.

What happened to Cassy, this enigma of a girl, his soulmate, his wife, the matriarch of their children and grandchildren? Why did she go insane? What did she see? What comes next? Once he awakened from this dream? Were there any answers? Was there a God?

"Grandpa? Knock, knock. Are you home?"

Ashwood opened his eyes. Birdie and the other two boys, Drake and Leo, were standing before him.

Ashwood blinked.

Birdie smiled. "Good. Our team has been talking and Leo had an interesting idea. But we need your advice. Okay?"

Ashwood blinked.

"Question: Who hung those last four paintings in the hallway? They're the same size and not that large. Was it you?"

Ashwood shut his eyes.

"Was it Grandma?"

Ashwood blinked.

Birdie showed excitement, glancing at the others. "Here is what we've been thinking. Leo, it was your idea. Tell him."

"Sir, I was—"

"Call him Grandpa," said Birdie.

"Grandpa," said Leo. "I was wondering if Grandma Cassy ever wrote on the backside of her paintings. Did she?"

Ashwood blinked.

"Did you happen to see if she wrote anything on the backside of these four paintings?"

Ashwood shut his eyes.

"We're thinking," said Birdie, "she might've left more clues."

Drake added, "Regarding, you know, the murders."

"If we're very careful," said Birdie, "would it be all right to take them off the wall and have a look?"

Ashwood hesitated a few seconds, then blinked.

Leo, being the tallest, lifted off the wall the painting with one tally mark. He turned it around and set it upright on the floor. Birdie, Drake, and Leo went down on their knees to have a closer look. Birdie had with her a round magnifying glass with a handle which she had removed from the library.

Drake said, "The back of a painting is called a verso. It's like the passport for a work of art, showing where it's been, and any details, credits and stuff."

"Look at that," said Leo. "Small writing along the center cross beam of the frame."

Birdie used the magnifying glass. "In capital letters. Maybe it's the painting's name? 'DUPLICITY.' And then smaller print... shit! She wrote, '*I was drugged with LSD, stripped naked, handcuffed to a sofa chair, and raped by Jimmy.*'"

"Oh, my God," said Drake. "Major discovery. What else?"

"There," said Leo. "She included numbers. 01/2001. Maybe the year it was painted?"

Drake consulted his notebook. It contained dates of the serial killings. "A month after this artist was killed. The first victim."

"Duplicity means deception," said Leo. "You know, pretending to feel and act one way while actually being just the opposite."

Birdie said, 'That portrait makes sense now. Explains why she painted a double exposure. Those two faces overlapping."

"Someone who's two-faced," said Leo, "Hiding a deceitful side while acting sincere. That's what that image is saying."

Birdie looked at the others. "Let's remove the next one."

Leo lifted the painting which showed a man's head sinking and dissolving inside a toilet bowl, with two tally marks at the bottom. He turned it around and set it beside the first painting.

He pointed. "There. The date: 03/2001."

Drake consulted his notebook. "Painted a month after this artist was killed. And there's more writing on the cross beam."

She held up the magnifying glass. "It says, 'PERFIDIOUS,' in all caps like the other one. What does that mean?"

"Same sentiment," said Leo. "Treachery, deceitfulness. What else did she write?"

Birdie looked back into the convex lens, then pulled away.

"Let me see." Leo took hold of the magnifying glass from Birdie and looked. "What the hell? She wrote, *'Luca sodomized me with a metal dildo.'*"

"That's sick," said Birdie. "Gross."

Drake said, "He was known for his art objects. He'd created a series of painted toilets. She was flushing him down a toilet. That's my take on the imagery."

Birdie said, "I'm not sure I'm ready for the next one."

Leo removed the painting with three tally marks, turning it over and setting it against the wall with the other two. The painting was dated similarly to the others: 06/2001.

Birdie said to Leo. "More writing. You read it."

"Weird. The title says, 'DEGRADATION.'"

"I'm afraid to know," said Birdie. "Go ahead, Leo. What?"

"She wrote, '*After I was raped and sodomized, Parker urinated all over me.*'"

"God! That is vile," said Drake. "Disgusting."

"Degradation," said Leo, "is the act of lowering someone to an inferior state, like having the beauty of something destroyed."

Drake said, "It does explain the Pollock-like squiggles of yellow, orange, and ochre paint covering the face in this portrait."

"Like she was pissings on *him*, said Leo."

Birdie was wiping away tears. "No wonder she went mad."

Leo looked at Birdie with concern. "Are you okay? Should we reveal the last one or not? It's up to you."

She nodded and Leo removed the fourth painting off the wall, setting it down along with the others.

"This one is dated 09/2001." Drake checked his notes. "Again, painted after this artist was murdered. What did she write?"

Leo shook his head. "A lot. First, 'DEMORALIZATION.' And then, '*Oscar took photos of me naked and defiled, to be made public if I told anyone what they did to me.*'"

Leo looked at the others. "There's more. Like a postscript? In very tiny letters."

"Read it," said Birdie.

"She wrote, '*Oscar was my best friend. He betrayed me. I don't know what to believe anymore. He shamed me. It has destroyed me. I have no control over what is happening. Now I have to die.*'"

Birdie, Drake, and Leo returned to stand before Ashwood who detected motion, being sensitive to sound, and opened his eyes.

"Leo was right," said Birdie. "Grandma Cassy wrote messages on the back of each painting about what happened to her that night. The night she went mad. Are you sure you want to hear this?"

Ashwood blinked.

"It's not good," said Birdie. "Drake copied down what she had written. Someone else has to read it. I can't."

"I will, Birdie," said Leo.

He took the notebook from Drake and began to read. As Birdie saw tears well up in her grandfather's eyes, she began to cry too, and walked away sobbing, unable to listen to how her grandmother had been savagely assaulted by people she once called friends.

CHAPTER 33

2001

Aaron had received a phone call from an art gallery informing him of the breaking news. He turned on the wall-mounted television rarely watched in the dining room to know more of what happened. Cassy's former flatmate, Jimmy, and co-founder of the Gang of Five art gallery had been found dead. He'd been murdered, stabbed in the heart, at the entrance of the studio warehouse. The police suspected the incident was a random robbery gone bad. His wallet and mobile phone were missing but nothing else.

The evening news showed a distraught woman, Lena, describing how she had found him. She was Jimmy's girlfriend, the reporter was told as she wiped away tears.

"I'm also a founding member of the Gang of Five."

"Liar," said Cassy to the television screen.

Lena continued, "Jimmy was a great artist, an innovator when it came to painting—"

"Not true," interjected Cassy. "What a crock."

"—and a wonderful, witty, generous man. He was not a violent person. He would have given the robber what he asked for and not put up a fight. He was a hippie, a man of peace."

"Aaron," said Cassy, "turn this off. I've heard enough."

"He was an asshole," said Blaise.

Aaron glanced at his son as he flicked off the television. "A man was murdered in cold blood. Show a little respect."

"He deserves none," said Cassy.

"How well did you know him, Mom?"

Cassy looked at Sky. Their family was seated around the dining room table on a Saturday night. Sky and Iris were eighteen years old, seniors in high school. Blaise was twenty-one years old, enrolled as a college student at UC Berkeley, living off campus but had driven across the bay on the weekend to make a home visit. Cassy glanced at Aaron before answering her daughter regarding her relationship to the murder victim.

"Not well at all, as it turned out."

Iris bit her lip, brow furrowed. "That woman looked like Lena, our nanny, who lived with us for awhile. Was it?"

"It did," said Sky. "She left when we were nine."

"Could that be her, Mom?"

"Yes, Iris," said Cassy. "But I don't want to talk about her."

"You never told us why she left," said Sky.

"I thought I knew *her* well too." Cassy lifted her fork, the tines spooled with pasta. "But I was wrong. Help me, Aaron."

"Lena became persona non grata." Aaron stood and held up the bottle of wine. "Alcohol is to drink casually and in moderation. It's a European tradition. Would you girls like a little wine?"

Both daughters raised their hands. Aaron poured them wine. He poured more for Cassy, Blaise, and himself. He sat in his chair.

"Girls," said Aaron, "your mom and I welcomed Lena into our home as a member of the family. But she violated our trust and did something bad. Inexcusable behavior. So we told her to leave."

Sky said, "What did she do that was so bad?"

"We're older now," said Iris. "You can tell us, Dad."

"No," said Cassy, "we can't."

Sky idly twirled pasta on her plate. "I hate family secrets. It's not healthy. We should be totally transparent."

"Totally," echoed Iris.

Cassy said, "Sorry girls that your dad and I are being opaque. But that's the way it has to be. End of subject."

Sky sulked. She looked at her brother. "Do you know why?"

Blaise drank wine and shook his head. "I haven't a clue."

"Okay, *whatever*." Sky sipped her wine. "What about Lena and this dead guy? If she turned out to be so bad, maybe she's somehow involved in his death. Who knows? She could be, right?"

"It wouldn't surprise me, Sky," said Cassy. "You never know what people are capable of doing to others.

Aaron approached Cassy, who was painting in her studio.

"You won't believe this." Aaron held up a newspaper. "I saw it while having my morning coffee. Guess who got murdered?"

Cassy swiveled on her stool, turning away from the easel. She dabbed her brush into paint on the pallete. "I give up. Who?"

"Luca. Stabbed in the heart. And same location as what's-his-name, Jimmy. Stolen wallet, phone, nothing else taken."

"Well, you did warn me that area wasn't safe."

"I did. Good thing you're not working there any longer."

"Good thing." Cassy swiveled back to her painting.

"It's sad. I always liked Luca. We got along quite well."

"Hum, well, shit happens."

"Cassy, I know you had a falling out with these guys but—"

"But what?"

"Nothing. You seem a little, I don't know."

"What?"

"Cold hearted. It's not like you. I thought you should know."

"Thanks for telling me."

Aaron stared at what Cassy was painting before leaving. "Is that a head sinking inside a toilet bowl?"

"It might be. I thought I'd experiment."

"Strange painting. By the way, the art galleries are calling. They keep asking about new paintings. What should I tell them?"

"That I've stopped selling my babies."

"Cassy, I understand, but—"

"Do you?"

"Yes. Every painting is important. They're special. But you've got finished artwork shelved in the walls. Filled to capacity. It's time to sell some of them."

"Why?"

"For one, it keeps you relevant."

Cassy swiveled around to face Aaron. "Relevant?"

"In the art world. As an artist. For the public to know you—"

"Still matter? To remain famous, you mean?"

"I'm only trying to help, Cassy."

"Like the way you thrust me into art exhibitions, giving endless interviews? To be relevant? Gain fame? Something I never wanted. And look where it got me! What it did to me!"

"That's bullshit! You loved the attention. And you wanted the recognition. Don't lie to yourself. And don't you *dare* make me feel guilty for promoting your artwork!"

Cassy swiveled on her stool away from Aaron, raising her brush to the canvas. "I only wanted to paint."

"I did it out of love for you. Because you're amazing."

Cassy swiveled back. "I'm not amazing. I'm a fucking wreck of a human being!"

"No you're not."

"Yes, I am. Look at me."

"Cassy, I don't know what happened to you that night. When you say you saw God. I'm sure it had to have been horrible."

"It was. But it wasn't God's fault. It was all mine."

"What do you mean?"

"Karma. For doing bad, stupid, selfish things. Like stealing and taking drugs. Acting reckless. I even killed a man, remember?"

"You told me. In self defense. You're still a good person."

"Am I?"

He came over and held her. She rested her head against his chest and closed her eyes.

"I just want it to end, Aaron. For it all to be over. Returning to the way we were."

"We'll get through this. I don't want us to fight. Okay?"

"Okay."

"Your babies are safe. We won't be selling them."

"Thank you."

They let go of each other, separating.

"I'm off to the city," said Aaron. "Are you all right?"

"Half right." She smiled. "Go."

"Kiss?"

Aaron leaned down. They kissed, then parted.

"Love you."

"Love you, too," said Cassy.

Three months later, Aaron was startled by the news of a third victim being murdered, another artist from the Gang of Five. Same details as the first two. Stabbed with a knife in the heart. Except at a different location. Two in the morning, at closing time, outside a bar that the victim frequented. The police were now considering this latest murder was connected to the work of a serial killer.

The art community had been stirred up with concern over the death of three renowned artists. Because each victim was associated with the Gang of Five art gallery, numerous calls were made, trying to reach Cassy for comments. Aaron fielded the phone calls and told the reporters his wife had no comment but, yes, he was concerned. As he hung up on the last caller, he returned to the dining room.

Cassy looked up from her salad. "Another one?"

"Norton," said Aaron. "Your friend at Artwalk magazine."

"Friend? Sort of. James has been surprisingly supportive after our awkward first encounter and has written glowing reviews about my paintings. I underestimated him. More wine, please."

"Aren't you worried, Mom?"

"What, Sky?"

"You should be worried," said Iris. "I am."

Aaron poured more wine into Cassy's empty glass.

"Thank you. No, girls. It's a bizarre coincidence. Besides, I have nothing to do with that art gallery any longer."

"Still," said Aaron. "It is cause for concern. Who knows what this serial killer is thinking. Does he hold a grudge against all artists? Or just them? I mean, Christ, what's his motive?"

"That art gallery screwed someone over," said Sky. "And he's out for revenge. That's my guess."

"He's a sicko," said Iris. "Did you tell Blaise?"

"No, Honey," said Cassy. "He's got enough on his mind with college courses and football season. Why distract him?"

"He *must* know," said Sky. "It's been all over the news."

Aaron said, "When I was in college I rarely listened to the news. It can be insular. Like living on an island."

"I'm surprised Blaise hasn't called," said Iris.

"I'll call him," said Aaron. He took hold of the plate passed to him with the pieces of chicken.

"Thanks for barbecuing tonight," said Cassy.

"My pleasure. I am curious though. After the first two from the Gang of Five were killed, did Parker or Oscar reach out to you?"

"Why would they?"

"Cassy, come on. You were one of the founders. You lived with those guys for how many years?"

"Seven, I think."

"Oscar was your close friend. And Parker—"

"Wasn't. We were never close. Besides, you know me, Aaron. And girls, you should too. I burn bridges when betrayed."

CHAPTER 34

2020

Ashwood saw his son staggering toward him. His daughters stopped him, each grabbing one of his arms. Words were exchanged. Blaise was causing a minor scene with family members looking on, all wondering, as was Ashwood, what was happening. Blaise gently yet forcefully removed himself from their restraint. He blew them a kiss, then held up his arms as if indicating for them to stay away. He stumbled backwards and turned, regaining his balance, weaving his way toward a nearby chair which he dragged across the hardwood floor, positioning it in front of Ashwood's wheelchair.

"Hi, Dad. Can I talk to you?"

Ashwood blinked.

"Sorry I've been missing in action. It's been awhile. I don't mean to be avoiding you. Business. The divorce. Getting Nora to remarry me. The family. Gets crazy raising kids. You know what I mean?"

Ashwood blinked.

"That's not what I came to talk to you about." Blaise rubbed his eyes before placing hands on his knees. "I'm a little drunk. I've been trying to get up the nerve to speak to you about something. Do you have any idea what I'm going to tell you?"

Ashwood shut his eyes.

Blaise looked away. "Oh, again, thanks for giving me that start up money. You saved me, Dad. Many times. I've tried to be a good son. I have. For you and Mom. I know I can be a pain in the ass. Nora makes that clear to me." He laughed. "It's true. But seriously, Dad. I never would have done the things I did if … I mean, Jesus. What happened to Mom. Damnit, this is hard."

Ashwood saw tears forming in Blaise's eyes.

"I lost my mind, Dad. It's why I dropped out of college. It's why

I got wasted in bars. I couldn't live with myself. I kept it all to myself bottled up. Because I had to. But I need to tell you. It's a confession, Dad. I'm responsible, I think, for killing Mom. I don't mean directly. Indirectly. Because of what I did. Do you have any idea what I'm talking about?"

Ashwood shut his eyes.

"I overheard what Birdie and the others discovered on the back of Mother's paintings. They must have told you. So now you know too. Those guys assaulted her. It was mean and brutal. I witnessed it all. I was supposed to be vacationing in Tahoe with Jason and his family. Remember my friend, Jason?"

Ashwood blinked.

"We came back early. Some emergency, so I got dropped off. I figured I'd surprise Mom. I went around back to the walkway to her studio. I heard a car coming up our gravel drive. I don't know why, but I hid, curious to see who it was. Then I saw her. It was *Lena*. And I thought, what the *fuck* is she doing here? Mom would never invite her back to the house. I watched as she walked to the front door and used a key to walk right in. It was stupid of me, but I snuck around the back, peering through the glass doors to see what was going on. I mean, considering what happened between us. It was weird that she'd be there. You know?"

Ashwood blinked.

"I'm sorry, again, for, you know. Anyway, I could see Mom was shocked to see her there. Uninvited, standing in our house. But, for some reason, they went into the kitchen, both returning with glasses of wine. They talked. I couldn't hear what they were saying. Then I heard another car coming up our driveway. I went and saw four guys getting out of a van. I got scared. I kind of panicked. I went back to watch from outside. You're going to hate me, Dad."

Ashwood closed his eyes briefly.

"No, you will. I did nothing to try and stop what happened to her. I was a fucking twelve-year-old coward." Blaise paused to wipe away tears. "Mom began freaking out, acting strange and shouting at them. She was scared. She even went to grab the switchblade kept in a drawer. It was knocked from her hand. She was pushed down onto the sofa. Dad, they tore off her clothes. Then Lena, this fucking *Lena*, she handcuffed Mom to the arms of the chair."

Ashwood watched as Blaise began sobbing.

"They drugged her, then raped and sodomized her. One of the men even urinated on her. To humiliate her. They wanted to destroy her. And they did. They took photos of her like that. Those bastards! I once swore to Mom I'd protect her. But I was a coward. That's why I killed them. I had to, for Mom's sake. Do you understand?"

Ashwood blinked.

"I did it for *Mom*. She'd never do it. So I had to. Except, she couldn't know. No one could. I wanted to kill Lena too, but I just couldn't bring myself to do it. I still loved her, Dad. I hated what she did to Mom. What we did to the family. I know I'm the one to blame for everything going to shit. And for Mom dying. I mean, Mom must have thought she was going to be murdered next. I don't know what she was thinking. But she disappeared. Because of me!"

Blaise dropped off the chair, falling to his knees, sobbing as he clutched his father's body.

"Forgive me, Dad. Please, forgive me. I'm sorry!"

Ashwood felt nothing physically, but he felt the pain of his son's anguish, along with his own, from this admission of guilt, as part of the family tragedy. Cassy often joked sarcastically, dismissively, that her maiden name, Crow, was cursed, considering what happened to her father, her brother, her mother. The family had gathered behind Blaise, listening to his breakdown and confession. Iris tapped her brother's shoulder, startling him. She handed him a napkin.

"Jesus, Blaise. It was you? You're the serial killer?"

ASHWOOD

CHAPTER 35

2001

Cassy had purchased the Volkswagen Beetle to be a surprise birthday gift for Lena. This was in 1992, and before she discovered Lena was having sex with her son. Lena's father restored used cars to make extra money, so Cassy approached him surreptitiously to make the arrangement, the transfer of cash. The father knew Cassy was Lena's employer and a famous painter. She desired anonymity, so he agreed to write his daughter's name as the new owner, which he submitted to the DMV. Cassy never bothered to register the car herself. She parked the vehicle in a self-storage rental unit, where it remained for ten years, unbeknownst to Aaron.

To avoid annoying monthly reminders of payments due, Cassy arranged with her bank to accept automatic monthly transactions for the rental charges to be deducted from a private savings account. At the time, Cassy thought the rental would last only months until Lena's birthday. But because of what transpired between Lena and their family, ten years had lapsed. She had forgotten about the car. Then it dawned on her one day that she possessed a car in storage. It was the beginning of a scenario she hatched in her mind after the news of Oscar's murder. The serial killer had stuck again and Cassy became seriously worried that she would be next.

The fourth painting in her series about the Gang of Five deaths was black, in memory of Oscar's minimalistic style. She cried with mixed emotions as she applied the paint onto the canvas. She was still in a quandary about their relationship, whether she'd been lied to and deceived, betrayed by her best friend, or self-deceived from ill-timed circumstances and assumptions she had made. Even if she *had* been wrong in making rash judgements, it didn't justify the savage attack on her by former flatmates whom she'd considered friends.

She felt the stab into her own heart as she poked a hole into the center of the black canvas, then painted a trail of blood. The red blood contrasted with the surrounding darkness, making it dramatic and metaphoric, expressing an ending to her profession as an artist. Except for the last painting she needed to create: her departure from this world. Cassy sensed her time on earth was coming to an end, so she painted the image fast, with a fury. The large painting was to be a reminder of who she was and what she hoped to become.

Words failed her. She painted images in lieu of words. Her final painting was more than just a suicide note. It was a love letter.

She would be the architect of her own demise. She refused to let a serial killer determine her fate. Cassy removed an article in a folder she'd saved about magicians. She was fascinated by illusions. Since her sexual assault, she had become perplexed by what was real and what wasn't. It was Houdini's death-defying stunts that inspired her to conceive of her own dramatic end to a new beginning.

Cassy was still haunted by the fact she had killed a man, even though it had been in self-defense. She believed in ghosts once she'd seen him appear during her drug-induced state after Lena had dosed her with a high quantity of LSD. She'd seen her mother and father. Her brother too, watching from another dimension.

Aaron, on the day they first met, told her he suspected there was something more beyond what humans could perceive.

To achieve what she intended, she had to overcome her worst fears, and accept death. Death was simply another dimension of life, she told herself. A feat she had to achieve on her own terms.

She was meticulous, accumulating the items she would need. Two tarps, a small camping shovel, a switchblade, and vodka for courage. She placed the items in the trunk of the Volkswagen Beetle. After ten years, the car was dead, unable to start. So she arranged for a gas station to replace the battery. Then she locked the storage shed. She needed to first finish her final painting called *Afterlife*.

Cassy was melancholy, but in a determined state of mind the morning she left her home. Personal identifying items, such as purse, mobile phone, credit cards, BMW, she left behind, taking only her driver's license and some cash. She walked to downtown Mill Valley disguised beneath a hat and dark glasses. She rode a cab that dropped her off at the storage unit containing her Beetle. If her plan failed and she was found, she mused about poetic justice, given that the vehicle was registered in Lena's name. She drove north to Oregon where she ended her journey at South Jetty Beach.

It was midweek, fall weather, overcast sky, and the beach was empty of crowds. Cassy was pleased she only saw a few people along the stretch of sand. She carried her bundle of essential items close to the water's edge. The tide was out but would rise at the end of the day. She laid out the two tarps, overlapping them slightly, aligning them horizontally with the shore. They formed a rectangular shape, the size of a grave. She unfolded the shovel, made an outline with its tip in the sand with the same dimensions as the tarps, and began to dig into the sand between the tarps and the ocean.

After a couple of hours, she had sand piled up onto the tarps. The rectangular hole was roughly two feet deep when a little girl wandered over to Cassy carrying a plastic pail and shovel.

"Can I play with you?"

Cassy, shovel in hand, looked at the child. "Oh. Hi."

"Are you building a sand castle?"

"I suppose I am," said Cassy.

"Can I help? I have a shovel. See?"

"I do. Sure, you can help me. Where are your parents?"

The girl pointed down the beach at distant figures. "Why are you putting all the sand up there. To build the sand castle?"

Cassy smiled and nodded.

"Is the hole for the water to surround the castle?"

"Yes, the moat. *Or*," said Cassy playfully "Maybe I'm digging a hole to reach the other side of the world."

The girl giggled. "No, you're not. That's not possible."

"You never know."

"You're silly. What's your name?"

"Cassy. What's yours?"

"Mia."

"That's a beautiful name. Do you want to know a secret?"

Mia nodded.

"I fell in love on this very beach. Years ago. Right here. Do you have a boyfriend, Mia?"

She shook her head.

"Someday you will. Falling in love is the most beautiful feeling you will ever experience here on earth."

Someone was shouting from far away down the beach.

"That's my mom calling." The girl got off her knees, placing her shovel in the pail. "Sorry, I have to go."

"So do I."

"Bye." The girl waved, then ran off.

"Bye." Cassy waved back.

At dusk, the beach was empty of people, the surf rising to touch the hole Cassy had dug. It was roughly four feet deep. Cassy sat on the edge of the grave, drinking from the flask of vodka. She had no idea if what she had planned would work. She'd seen a similar stunt on a television show called Fear Factor, or some name like that. She had spread the pile of sand evenly across both tarps. Upon finishing the vodka, she sat into the hole, placed the shovel and knife to her side. She tugged on the furthest tarp covered with the layers of sand.

It was heavier and harder to move than she'd imagined. But she was finally able to pull it on top of her lower half. The weight across her legs was heavy. She used the shovel to spread and smooth the sand so that it aligned with the surrounding sand. She placed the shovel to her side, the knife on her lap, held her breath and tugged at the other tarp. As the sand started to spill onto her, she yanked hard. The tarp and sand collapsed like an avalanche on top of her.

Cassy was stunned by the pressure of it. She struggled to move her arm, to find the switchblade and stab herself through the heart. She could barely move. It was her worst nightmare. But she relented, suffering for her sins. She envisioned the Catholic school with all the murals and statues of Jesus looking down while crucified on a cross. She cried, thinking of her family, who loved her, and whom she was leaving behind. She felt salt water mixing with her tears as the rising ocean tide washed over her and into the crevices of the hole she had dug. She was inebriated, shivering, suffocating.

Her suicide had not gone as planned. After a few minutes, she drowned, buried alive.

ASHWOOD

CHAPTER 36

2020

Ashwood watched as Blaise was helped up and brought to sit on the sofa. He was surrounded by a stunned family still processing his confession that he had killed the four artists. His hands shook as he drank from a mug of coffee Bill had offered him.

Sky asked, "What knife did you use, Blaise? Mom's?"

"Her switchblade? No, I had my own. Had it for years."

"So where is it now?"

"At the bottom of the San Francisco Bay, Sky."

Iris asked, "What other skeletons are hiding in your closet?"

Blaise looked up at his sisters, still standing. He gazed around at everyone staring at him – his wife, son, daughter, sisters, brothers-in-law, nephews, nieces, and Birdie's guest.

"I'm the reason Lena was told to leave our house."

"Do tell, Brother," said Sky.

"Dad caught us having sex late one night."

"No," said Iris, seating herself.

"Yes," said Blaise.

"But," said Sky. "You were just a kid."

"Twelve. Old enough."

"To know better," said Iris.

"Not really," said Blaise. "She did, maybe. But I loved her."

"You were *twelve*," said Sky. "It was *lust*, not love."

"Either way." Blaise sipped his coffee. "That's why I couldn't bring myself to kill her. She did participate in the assault on Mom, by drugging her. But, since she was my first love, I couldn't do it. That's it. No more skeletons to bring out and share, I swear."

"Well," said Iris, "that's a small relief."

He looked at his wife. "Please don't divorce me again."

"Not for *that*." Nora had the hint of a smile.

Blaise set the coffee mug on the table. He raked fingers through his hair, closed his eyes, shook his head. "Now what do I do? Turn myself into the police? Make a full confession? Anyone?"

"No," said Birdie to everyone's surprise. "Those men tortured Grandma and got what they deserved. They're the reason she went crazy, disappeared, and is dead. Uncle Blaise, I don't blame you for going crazy too and doing what you did."

"I agree," said Sky. "How does everyone else feel?"

Blaise saw them responding with nods and muttering words of assent. He began to cry. "I wish Mom was alive. I blame myself for her death. I just wanted to help her and for her to be proud of me. Not for her to take her own life, assuming that's what she did."

"We'll never know," said Sky.

"I guess it will remain an unsolved mystery," said Iris.

"Maybe that's what Grandma Cassy wanted."

Her father asked, "What do you mean by that, Birdie?"

"To be remembered as an unsolved mystery."

Ashwood looked from his family up to the painting on the wall. Cassy's angel. *Afterlife.* He saw the angel rising, moving toward him. He shut his eyes. He couldn't keep them open any longer. His body was feeling the weight of time. The gravity of living.

He felt the allure. Euphoria. That was the sensation of pleasure he was feeling. The warmth of her sparkling face. Her smile full of love. Her appearance hovering before him dreamlike, pressing her lips into his. He knew it was Cassy as she embraced him, wrapping her limbs around him lovingly, like a transcendent octopus, lifting him away, rising together into a luminous liquid blue sky.

www.ingramcontent.com/pod-product-compliance
Lightning Source LLC
LaVergne TN
LVHW061529070526
838199LV00009B/426